West Indian Americans

Recent Titles in
Bibliographies and Indexes in Afro-American and African Studies

A Bibliographical Guide to African-American Women Writers
Casper LeRoy Jordan, compiler

Invisible Wings: An Annotated Bibliography on Blacks in Aviation, 1916–1993
Betty Kaplan Gubert, compiler

The French Critical Reception of African-American Literature: From the Beginnings to
1970, An Annotated Bibliography
*Michel Fabre, compiler, with the assistance of Rosa Bobia, Christina Davis, Charles
Edwards O'Neill, and Jack Salzman*

Zora Neale Hurston: An Annotated Bibliography and Reference Guide
Rose Parkman Davis, compiler

Roots of Afrocentric Thought: A Reference Guide to Negro Digest/
Black World, 1961–1976
Clovis E. Semmes, compiler

African American Criminologists, 1970–1996: An Annotated Bibliography
Lee E. Ross, compiler

Contemporary African American Female Playwrights: An Annotated Bibliography
Dana A. Williams

Rooted in the Chants of Slaves, Blacks in the Humanities, 1985–1997: A Selectively
Annotated Bibliography
Donald Franklin Joyce, compiler

The African-American Male: An Annotated Bibliography
Jacob U. Gordon, compiler

Blacks in the American West and Beyond—America, Canada, and Mexico: A Selectively
Annotated Bibliography
George H. Junne, Jr.

Bibliography of African American Leadership: An Annotated Guide
Ronald W. Walters and Cedric Johnson

African American Women: An Annotated Bibliography
Veronica G. Thomas, Kisha Braithwaite, and Paula Mitchell, compilers

West Indian Americans

A Research Guide

Guy T. Westmoreland, Jr.

Bibliographies and Indexes in Afro-American and African Studies,
Number 43

GREENWOOD PRESS
Westport, Connecticut • London

E
184
.W54
W47
2001

Library of Congress Cataloging-in-Publication Data

Westmoreland, Guy T.
     West Indian Americans : a research guide / Guy T. Westmoreland, Jr.
        p. cm.—(Bibliographies and indexes in Afro-American and African studies, ISSN
     0742–6925 ; no. 43)
     Includes bibliographical references and indexes.
     ISBN 0–313–29792–4 (alk. paper)
     1. West Indian Americans—Bibliography.   I. Title.   II. Series.
     Z1361.W45 W47   2001
     [E184.W54]
     016.97304'96972—dc21   00–052109

British Library Cataloguing in Publication Data is available.

Library of Congress Catalog Card Number: 00–052109
ISBN: 0–313–29792–4
ISSN: 0742–6925

First published in 2001

Greenwood Press, 88 Post Road West, Westport, CT 06881
An imprint of Greenwood Publishing Group, Inc.
www.greenwood.com

Printed in the United States of America

The paper used in this book complies with the
Permanent Paper Standard issued by the National
Information Standards Organization (Z39.48–1984).

10 9 8 7 6 5 4 3 2 1

45330224

To all Descendants of the Forced African Diaspora

Contents

Introduction   ix

1. Background Studies and Reference Sources
   Background Studies   1
   Reference Sources   4

2. Community Life
   General Studies   9
   Crime   14
   Cultural Activities   16
   West Indian American Day Carnival   18

3. Economic Life
   General Studies   23
   Farm Labor   34
   Women in the Economy   37

4. Education   41

5. Ethnicity and Race Relations   53

6. Family Relationships   69

7. Health Care   75

8. Immigration and Settlement Patterns   83

9. Politics   101

Author Index   113

Title Index   119

Subject Index   137

Introduction

With the passage of the 1965 Immigration and Nationality Act, United States immigration policy changed from emphasizing European immigration to permitting more immigration from Asia, Africa, South American and the Caribbean. Since that time, large numbers of Caribbean people have sought improved economic advantages by migrating to the United States. As citizens of structurally underdeveloped societies, thousands in the Caribbean region face not only unemployment but also chronic underemployment in economies that depend primarily on agricultural exports and tourism. Therefore, many Caribbean nationals seek a better life in the United States.

This guide concentrates on immigrants to the United States from the English-speaking Caribbean and Haiti. Many scholars maintain that the underdeveloped status of these Caribbean regions results from their history as former slave-based, agricultural societies and that this underdevelopment has led to mass migration to the United States. From the 15th to the 19th century, an odious global trading system flourished wherein England and France exchanged minor manufactured goods on the coast of Africa for human chattel. In the West Indies, this captive labor force was used to create one-crop agricultural societies based primarily on the production of sugar, molasses, tobacco, or coffee for export to Europe and North America. Historically, sugar was the dominant and extremely valuable export crop. Thus, great wealth was created for the economies of Great Britain, France, and elements in the Northern United States. The European maritime powers of Britain and France grew to be industrial powers with the major influx of profits derived from the forced, unpaid labor of Africans transported to the Caribbean.

Over one and a half million African slaves landed in the British-speaking Caribbean between the 15th and 19th centuries. In 1789 Haiti (Saint Domingue at the time), there were 500,000 slaves with 30,000 more arriving annually. These captives produced a few staple crops on a massive scale. The agricultural output of these laborers was shipped to European metropolitan centers for processing and distribution. In turn manufactured goods, produced in North America and Europe, were shipped to the West Indies to sustain slave societies. These societies never developed self-sustaining economic infrastructures and quickly became dependent on the industrializing metropolis for most manufactured goods, foodstuffs, and capital.

British navigation laws insured that its colonies served as exporters of raw products to Europe, where they were processed into finished products. Manufacturing in the slave-based economies was expressly discouraged. Therefore, the West Indies quickly became dependent upon Britain and other European societies for the income to purchase manufactured goods and the actual supply of those goods.

Profits from the sugar plantations enabled many economically modest adventurers to establish rich dynasties, created a powerful class of wealthy absentee owners, and ultimately provided one of the largest transfers of capital in Britain's history. Thus the Caribbean sugar economies were characterized by technological stagnation which prevented development. It can be argued that underdevelopment was fostered because technological change in the dominant industry reduced the economic integration of an already fragmented local Caribbean economy.

In the case of Haiti, revolution and autonomous political development required the destruction of the export-oriented plantation economy. Left without sources of export income (sugar or coffee), the newly independent state lacked the means to fuel autonomous economic development. The ultimate outcome was a peasant-based underdeveloped economy, which moved into the dependent sphere of the United States.

Today, these societies remain primarily underdeveloped economic dependencies of the United States. Faced with large percentages of unemployment and underemployment, many Caribbean citizens seek economic advantage by migrating to the United States. This migratory flow has made major impacts on urban areas in the United States, especially in New York, Florida, and California. These post-1965 immigrants have dramatically changed New York City and Miami, Florida where many urban neighborhoods have been reborn as Caribbean enclaves.

As a result, many urban school districts have faced the challenges of new students with unfamiliar linguistic, social, and cultural characteristics. Various employment sectors, including health and home care, have seen dramatic increases in the percentage of employees from the West Indies. Caribbean religious practices, restaurants, grocery stores, and economic support groups have changed the culture of many urban neighborhoods. These immigrants have also added new dimensions to America's ethnic/racial dynamics and its political and economic life.

This guide organizes and annotates a significant portion of the significant body of studies that explore the impact of West Indian Americans on American society and of American society on the immigrants themselves. The goal is to concentrate on studies beneficial to college students as sources of information for selected research efforts and as possible leads for further investigation. My goal has been to indicate the direction and scope of past research efforts rather than to list every available study. Furthermore, this guide in no way attempts to chronicle individual West Indian Americans; it concentrates on studies that consider group impact. In some cases, studies of individuals are included as representative of special achievements, movements, or overall cultural impact.

Chapter 1, "Background Studies and Reference Sources," describes several studies that give historical context to this immigrant movement and reference works valuable for related facts and statistics. The balance of the guide is devoted to studies on West Indian American community and economic life, education, ethnicity and race relations, family relationships, health care, immigration and settlement patterns, and politics. I hope the studies presented will give a meaningful picture of the impact of West Indian migration on America and the impact of the immigration experience on the transformed immigrants and their descendants.

It should be emphasized that all descriptions of these studies are attempts to convey the opinions/conclusions of their authors and not of this compiler. I am sure that many of the findings and opinions have the potential to generate controversy and disagreement. My goal has been to report their conclusions and not to indicate any personal agreement or disagreement with them.

Most of the studies listed are readily available in college and/or university libraries, major public libraries, or through interlibrary loan/document delivery services offered by such libraries. Material has been drawn primarily from articles in professional/scholarly journals, books, dissertations and research reports as well as substantial articles in general interest magazines and newspapers. Also included are several authoritative Internet World Wide Web sites primarily with the Reference Sources. Conference proceedings are generally not included, as they are often difficult for undergraduates to obtain.

Dissertations are included because they can be an especially rich source of relevant and specific studies. The short annotations provided can be supplemented by obtaining longer summaries from the Dissertation Abstracts International database. Copies of dissertations can be consulted in the library of the institution that awarded the degree. However, dissertations published after 1957 are generally not available through interlibrary loan services. Those who desire to purchase one or more dissertations can do so by contacting Bell and Howell (formerly UMI) in Ann Arbor, Michigan. Reference librarians can provide further assistance in obtaining dissertation order numbers from the DAI database and Bell and Howell/UMI contact information.

Another type of document cited is ERIC (Educational Resources Information Center) Reports. The citations to the reports include "ED" numbers. The "ED" number is the identifying key to these reports on microfiche. Many college and university or large public libraries have collections of ERIC documents available on microfiche for consultation or photocopying. In addition, hard copies of these documents may be ordered from the ERIC Document Reproduction Service. Once again, reference librarians can assist in obtaining copies of the documents.

In compiling this guide, I had the invaluable assistance of the Interlibrary Loan/Document Delivery services of the City College of the City University of New York Library. Through that unit's efforts, I obtained copies of a large percentage of the items cited and described in this guide. This project also benefited significantly from the editorial skills of my former colleague, City College of New York Professor Emeritus Barbara J. Dunlap. Despite Professor Dunlap's efforts, I am responsible for any errors remaining in this publication.

Chapter 1

Background Studies and Reference Sources

BACKGROUND STUDIES

101.   Berlin, Ira. "The Structure of the Free Negro Caste in the Antebellum United States." *Journal of Social History* 9, no. 3 (1976): 297-318. Discusses how various patterns of emancipation and other circumstances created distinct castes of free African Americans in the North and the Upper and Lower South. The Lower South saw significant immigration of free Haitian mulattos, who fled Haiti's slave rebellion between 1790-1810. Their wealth, light skin color, and West Indian origins enabled them to establish a thriving economic caste apart from rural black slaves of the region.

102.   Bogen, Elizabeth. *Caribbean Immigrants in New York City: A Demographic Summary*. New York: Dept. of City Planning, Office of Immigrant Affairs and Population Analysis Division, 1988. A demographic analysis of New York City's West Indian population, based on the 1980 United States Census. Includes a brief history of West Indian immigration to New York City back to 1900. Statistical tables analyze West Indian nationality groups by three periods of immigration to the United States and by New York City borough of residence. Other statistics consider family economic and employment characteristics. Includes a map of "New York City Community Districts with more than 5,000 Caribbean-born Immigrants, 1980."

103.   Domingo, W. A. "The Tropics in New York." *The Survey: Social, Charitable, Civic: A Journal of Constructive Philanthropy* 53 (1925): 648-650. Discusses the impact of West Indian immigrants on 1920s Harlem and new influences that caused West Indians to adopt a Caribbean identity not bound by their island origins. These middle, artisan, and working class immigrants played major roles in the skilled trades, professions and business. Cultural differences led to friction with native African Americans and a refusal to accept America's rigid color line.

104.   Holder, Calvin B. "The Causes and Composition of West Indian Immigration to New York City, 1900-1952." *Afro-Americans in New York Life and History* 11, no. 1 (1987): 7-21. Natural disasters and poor economic prospects in the Caribbean are described as the primary cause of West Indian migration to the United States from 1900 to 1952. New York City's economic conditions and the perception of a favorable racial climate (though the opposite often proved to be the case) were primary attractions for professional and skilled West Indians.

105.   Laguerre, Michel S. "Haitians." In *Harvard Encyclopedia of American Ethnic Groups*, edited by Stephan Thernstrom, et al., 446-449. Cambridge, Mass.: Belknap Press of Harvard University Press, 1980. Surveys Haitian migration to the United States from 1791 through the 1970s. The Haitian Revolution, 1791-1803, caused many Haitian free blacks as well as white planters and their slaves to flee to New York and other American cities. Later, Haitians actively participated in the Harlem Renaissance and the Marcus Garvey movement (1915-1934). From 1957 into the 1970s, Haitian neighborhoods in New York City reproduced the social stratification of Port-au-Prince; former peasants struggled to advance; middle-class Haitians retreated to their subculture; and politics centered on Haiti.

106.   Marshall, Dawn I. "The History of Caribbean Migrations: The Case of the West Indies." *Caribbean Review* 11 (1982): 6-9, 52-53. Surveys four periods of Caribbean Migration, beginning with 1835-1885 (an inter-territorial period). Although the 1885-1920 period was primarily inter-Caribbean it resulted from United States investments in the Caribbean. Estimates of Caribbean migration to the United States between 1904 and 1914 are also noted. The relevance of United States immigration legislation and the recruitment of contract labor are highlights of the post-1940 period.

107.   Ottley, Roi, and William J.Weatherby. "Echoes of Haitian Thunder." Chap. 4 in *The Negro in New York: An Informal Social History*, edited by Roi Ottley and William J. Weatherby, 43-56. Dobbs Ferry, N.Y.: Oceana Publications, 1967. The 1791 Haitian Revolution was the catalyst for the earliest flow of black immigrants to New York City from the Caribbean. Many black slaves were forced to accompany white refugees from the Haitian revolt and many black survivors of punitive French massacres stowed away on ships that called at Haiti during the revolution.

108.   Ottley, Roi, and William J. Weatherby. "New Faces." Chap. 12 in *The Negro in New York: An Informal Social History*, edited by Roi Ottley and William J. Weatherby, 179-194. Dobbs Ferry, N.Y.: Oceana Publications, 1967. By the mid-1800s, foreign-born blacks began settling in New York City. Voluntary migration between 1919 and 1929 added a significant number of black immigrants from Haiti, Guadeloupe, Martinique, and the then British West

Indies to Harlem's population. West Indian migrants' trades and professions, savings habits, ethnic/race relations, and fraternal organizations are described.

109.   Portes, Alejandro, and Ramon Grosfoguel. "Caribbean Diasporas: Migration and Ethnic Communities." *Annals of the American Academy of Political and Social Science* 533 (1994): 48-69. Surveys the migration flows to the United States of five Caribbean national groups, including Jamaicans and Haitians, during the 20th century. Finds that United States' hegemony over these island nations subsequently affected their respective migration flows and success of their immigrant communities. Statistical tables included reflect the topics explored regarding these groups: (1) Migration by Decades; (2) Immigrant Occupations, 1969-90; (3) Immigrant Populations by State, 1980 and 1990; and (4) Immigrant Socioeconomic Characteristics, 1980.

110.   Reid, Ira De A. *The Negro Immigrant: His Background, Characteristics and Social Adjustment, 1899-1937.* 1939. Reprint, New York: AMS Press, 1968. A classic exploration of the impact of United States culture on West Indian migrants to New York City as of the 1930s. Also analyzes the impact of Caribbean cultures upon native black Americans and the resulting cultural and racial clashes. Finds that conflicts between black immigrants and native born blacks caused immigrant culture to disintegrate, with the immigrant assuming many native black cultural norms and folkways. Population of the black immigrant and native black population, by New York City borough for 1930, are among the statistical tables included.

111.   Reimers, David M. "Recent Third World Immigration to New York City, 1945-1986: An Overview." Chap. 8 in *Immigration to New York*, edited by William Pencak, et al., 179-197. Cranbury, N.J.: Associated University Presses, 1991. Outlines Caribbean immigration to New York City from the 1790s, to 1900 and 1945-1986. This flow increased from 1945 to 1965 and to a greater extent with the 1965 passage of federal immigration legislation so that by 1985, West Indians were 30 percent of the city's foreign-born population. Migration from Trinidad/Tobago and Jamaica resulted in New York City having the largest United States Jamaican population by 1980.   By 1985 Haitians had become the largest undocumented group and were concentrated at the low end of the economy.

112.   Ueda, Reed. "West Indians." In *Harvard Encyclopedia of American Ethnic Groups*, edited by Stephan Thernstrom, et al., 1020-1027. Cambridge, Mass.: Belknap Press of Harvard University Press, 1980. Surveys West Indian immigration to the United States from 1900 to the 1970s. By the 1930s New York City contained 65 percent of all immigrant blacks and despite discrimination West Indians in Harlem had strong rotating credit associations and businesses. Politics centered on Marcus Garvey's movement (1915-1934), while 1930s community life centered on over 30 mutual benefit associations and

the church. Professionals and skilled workers dominated the immigrant pool into mid-century and by the 1970s over 50 percent of the city's black businesses were owned by West Indians.

113.   Walter, John C. "The Caribbean Immigrant Impulse in American Life." *Revista Interamericana* 11 (1981-82): 522-544. Despite restrictive United States immigration policies, from 1915 to 1930, black immigrants constituted 5.2 percent of the United States population by 1930. The literacy requirements for immigration resulted in the well-educated Caribbean immigrants soon dominating black America's professional, business, cultural, and political leadership. By 1930, New York City was host to most immigrant blacks and West Indians led black participation in the Socialist, Communist, and trade union movements and in Harlem's cultural flowering. While West Indians' tendency to retain their British citizenship led to animosity with native blacks, government harassment of Caribbean agitators tended to decrease this animosity.

114.   Watkins-Owens, Irma. *Blood Relations: Caribbean Immigrants and the Harlem Community, 1900-1930*. Bloomington: Indiana University Press, 1996. Explores the impact of some 40,000 black Caribbean immigrants to Harlem, between 1900 and 1930, and the resultant interracial ethnic dimensions of community life. Also discusses the friction between native-born blacks and West Indians and the contributions of West Indians to the political and business life of Harlem.

REFERENCE SOURCES

115.   Brana-Shute, Rosemary, and Rosmarijn Hoefte. *A Bibliography of Caribbean Migration and Caribbean Immigrant Communities*. Gainesville, Fla.: University of Florida Libraries, 1983. A comprehensive listing of over 2500 references on migration within the Caribbean and overseas to metropolitan centers. A wide variety of published and unpublished sources, in several languages, cover varying aspects of acculturation and impact on receiving societies. Non-annotated entries are arranged alphabetically by author. Three of the appendices index entries by migrant origins (e.g., island or region), migrant destination (e.g., country or city) and topics such as urbanization and women.

116.   Center for Afro-American and African Studies. *Black Immigration and Ethnicity in the United States: An Annotated Bibliography*. Westport, Conn.: Greenwood Press, 1985. Various publications are listed and selectively annotated in this broad survey of black ethnicity and immigration. Topically organized by broad categories including United States immigration legislation and policies; historical, socioeconomic and literary aspects of black immigration; and black immigrant groups from Africa and the Caribbean. Includes author and subject indexes.

117.   Cordasco, Francesco. *The New American Immigration: Evolving Patterns of Legal and Illegal Emigration: A Bibliography of Selected References*. New York: Garland Publishing, 1987. Lists over 2000 bibliographic and institutional (e.g., museums and libraries) sources on immigration to the United States with an index covering authors and institutions. The entries, many with annotations, are grouped in three major sections: (1) American Immigration Before 1965, (2) American Immigration After 1965, and (3) Illegal Immigrants in the United States. While lacking a subject index, included is a lengthy outline of the history of American immigration policy from the Chinese Exclusion Act of 1882 to the Immigration Reform and Control Act of 1986.

118.   Hellman, Ronald G., and Beth K. Pfannl, eds. *Tinker Guide to Latin American and Caribbean Policy and Scholarly Resources in Metropolitan New York*. New York: Bildner Center, Graduate School and University Center, The City University of New York, 1988. A descriptive compilation of various New York City area organizations with collections and activities related to Latin America and the Caribbean. The size, overall strength, and subject specialization of library and research center collections is noted. Information on associations and research centers also includes their purpose, activities/fields of research, research facilities, and publications.

119.   Laidlaw, Walter, ed. *Population of the City of New York, 1890-1930*. Compiled and edited by Walter Laidlaw, Executive Secretary. New York: Cities Census Committee, Inc., 1932. Presents detailed population statistics for New York City and its region at each ten-year interval from 1890 to 1930. One of the volume's six sections presents statistics by "Nativity and Color." A particularly useful table therein deals with nativity of the foreign-born and provides data on migrants from Cuba and the West Indies.

120.   Lawless, Robert. *Haiti: A Research Handbook*. New York: Garland Publishing, 1990. A non-annotated listing of articles, books and other material on Haiti from both Creole and English sources. Initial chapters list sources on Haitian history by nine chronological periods. Other chapters organize references by cultural, socioeconomic, health, and science issues. A chapter on migration includes over 125 entries dealing with various aspects of Haitian migration within Haiti and abroad to metropolitan centers.

121.   Levinson, David, and Melvin Ember. *American Immigrant Cultures: Builders of a Nation*. 2 vols. New York: Simon & Schuster Macmillan, 1997. A solid reference work on non-indigenous cultural groups in the United States. It covers each group's culture, including immigration and settlement histories, language, economic patterns, housing, religion, marriage, family, and inter-ethnic relations. Includes an appendix of demographic data. Includes coverage of six West Indian nationalities.

122.   Mollenkopf, John H. *New York City in the 1980s: A Social, Economic, and Political Atlas.* New York: Simon & Schuster, 1993. A collection of maps, charts, and tables integrated into sections that explore the social, economic, and political changes in 1980s New York City. The first section, "Race, Income, and Immigration," includes maps on black population change, 1980-1990; West Indian and black population, 1980-1990; and West Indian ancestry population, 1990. Social-economic and health issues are discussed and illustrated in section two. Section three, on political participation, includes maps illustrating ethnic groups and political party registration by State Assembly districts. Appendix tables include "Industry of Employment by Ethnic Group, 1990" and "Occupation by Ethnic Group, 1990."

123.   National Coalition for Haitian Rights. *National Coalition for Haitian rights.* [Online] http://www.nchr.org/.   An Internet Web site outlining the activities of the NCHR, which works to increase the political effectiveness of the Haitian-American community. NCHR also organizes support for human rights in Haiti. A community bulletin board lists related national and local New York City events.

124.   Salvo, Joseph J. *The Newest New Yorkers: An Analysis of Immigration into New York City During the 1980s.* New York: New York Dept. of City Planning, 1992. Uses United States Immigration and Naturalization Service and Census Bureau data to profile migrants who attained permanent United States residency status and lived in New York City between 1982 and 1989. In some cases, migration data covers 1965 to 1989. Age, sex, marital status, and occupation profile immigrants from major source countries. Also presents basic immigrant counts, by country of birth, for neighborhoods in all city boroughs. Borough maps and charts indicate immigrant distribution by zip code. Total numbers of immigrants, by country of origin, are illustrated for 1850-1990.

125.   Segal, Aaron. *An Atlas of International Migration.* London; New York: Hans Zell Publishers, 1993. Includes a combination of maps and texts on global and regional migration from the origins of humans to the late 20th century. Maps present historical and contemporary migration trends for refugees, legal and illegal immigrants.

126.   U.S. Dept. of Commerce. Bureau of the Census. *1990 Census of Population. Ancestry of the Population in the United States.* (Internet Site) Washington, D.C.: U.S. Dept. of Commerce, Economic and Statistics Administration, Bureau of the Census, 1990. [Online] http://www.census.gov/population/www/-ancestry.html. Statistical data on selected ancestry groups by nativity, citizenship, and year of entry to the United States. In most series, there is one report for each state plus a national summary. Among the characteristics covered in seven statistical series are household and family; social (e.g., educational attainment); labor force; income and poverty; and housing.

127.   U.S. Dept. of Commerce, Bureau of the Census. *The Foreign-Born Population* (Internet Site). Washington, D.C.: U.S. Dept. of Commerce, Bureau of the Census, 1999. By Laura K. Yax, Population Division, U.S. Bureau of the Census. [Online] http://blue.census.gov/population/www/socdemo/foreign.html. Contains sample data, statistically weighted for totals, on migrants from various regions and countries of the world who are citizens and non-citizens of the United States. Place of birth designations for migrants from the Americas are included. As of 1999, data was available for 1994 through 1997. Detailed statistics are available in categories of Jamaican and other Caribbean foreign born.

128.   U.S. Dept. of Commerce, Bureau of the Census. *Historical Statistics on the Foreign-Born Population of the United States: 1850 to 1990* (Internet Site). Washington, D.C.: U.S. Dept. of Commerce, Bureau of the Census, 1999. By Campbell Gibson and Emily Lemon, Population Division, U.S.Bureau of the Census. [Online] http://www.census.gov/population/www/documentation/-twps0029/ twps0029.html. A working paper, which presents selected decennial census data on the foreign-born population of the United States from 1850 to 1990. Of particular interest are Table 3, Region and Country of Birth... and Table 5, Language Spoken at Home...

129.   U.S. Dept. of Commerce, Economic and Statistics Administration, Bureau of the Census. *Statistical Abstract of the United States*. Washington, D.C.: U.S. Government Printing Office, 19--. [Online] http://www.census.gov/-statab/www/. An annual, official summary of statistics on the social, political, and economic organization of the United States. Includes selected data from many statistical publications, both governmental and private. Among the immigration statistics included are the foreign-born population by place of birth in an individual year and over a range of years.

130.   U.S. Dept. of Commerce. Bureau of the Census. *Selected Characteristics for Persons of British West Indian Ancestry: 1990* (Internet Site). Washington, D.C.: U.S. Dept. of Commerce. Bureau of the Census, 1998. [Online] http://blue.census.gov/population/socdemo/ancestry/-British_West_Indian.txt. Valuable statistics on West Indian Americans of British ancestry, covering topics such as age and sex, nativity and year of entry, marital status, fertility, households' size, educational attainment, and linguistic ability.

131.   U.S. Dept. of Commerce. Bureau of the Census. *Selected Characteristics for Persons of Dutch West Indian Ancestry: 1990* (Internet Site). Washington, D.C.: U.S. Dept. of Commere. Bureau of the Census, 1998. [Online] http://blue.census.gov/population/socdemo/ancestry/-Dutch_West_Indian.txt. Presents demographic and socioeconomic statistics for Americans of Dutch West Indian Ancestry.

132.   U.S. Dept. of Justice, Immigration and Naturalization Service. *Immigration and Naturalization Statistics.* (Internet Site). Washington, D.C.: U.S. Dept. of Justice, Immigration and Naturalization Service, [Online] http://www.ins.usdoj.gov/graphics/aboutins/statistics/index.htm. A detailed annual compilation of statistics on immigration to the United States, retrospective to 1994. Also included are state estimates of the United States illegal alien resident and foreign-born populations. An overview of the legislative history of immigration to the United States is available in the agency's *Statistical Yearbook* (included).

133.   U.S. Dept. of Justice, Immigration and Naturalization Service, Statistics Division. *Immigration Fact Sheet.* (Internet Site). Washington, D.C.: U.S. Dept. of Justice, Immigration and Naturalization Service, [Online] http://www.ins.-usdoj.gov/graphics/aboutins/statistics/110.htm. A compilation of recent statistics and historical data on national origin and residence of immigrants and the foreign-born population in the United States.

134.   U.S. Dept. of State, Bureau of Security and Consular Affairs. *Report of the Visa Office* (Internet Site). [Online] http://travel.state.gov/visa_services.html. Washington, D.C.: U.S. Dept. of State, Bureau of Security and Consular Affairs. Provides a statistical picture of visas granted, by fiscal year, for entrance to the United States. Charts and tables include data on immigration by geographic area.

135.   University of California, Davis. *Migration News* (Internet Site). [Online] http://migration.ucdavis.edu/mn/mntxt.html. Summarizes the most important immigration and integration developments of the preceding month. Topics are grouped by region: North America, Europe, Asia, and other. Retrospective coverage to 1994.

Chapter 2

Community Life

GENERAL STUDIES

201.   Alexander, Daryl A. "For Thanksgiving, Two Feasts Two Traditions; A Spicy Blend of Caribbean and Black-American Flavors." *The New York Times* (19 November 1986): 1. Sect.C, Col.1. Caribbean and American traditions are blended in distinctive Thanksgiving Day dinners prepared by West Indians in Brooklyn, New York.

202.   Armand, Yolaine Pierre-Noel. "The Persistence of Status in Social Stratification: A Case Study of Haitian Society." Ph.D. Dissertation, New School for Social Research (New York), 1988. The researcher observes that there are two patterns of social stratification in Haiti and among Haitians in the New York City area. The patterns are "class stratification," based on such factors as income and education, and "status stratification," factors of prestige and social recognition of worth. Status is observed to cut across occupational and income boundaries and to have persisted among Haitians in Haiti and in the New York City area.

203.   Basch, Linda. "The Vincentians and Grenadians: The Role of Voluntary Associations in Immigrant Adaptation to New York City." Chap. 6 in *New Immigrants in New York*, edited by Nancy Foner, 159-193. New York: Columbia University Press, 1987. Voluntary associations enabled immigrants from St. Vincent and Grenada to impact New York City and to adjust to what they determined to be a hostile, racially and ethnically charged environment. The environment encouraged clustering in West Indian enclaves of Brooklyn where voluntary associations reinforced cultural identity, especially their uniqueness from native black Americans. Associations also linked these groups emotionally, politically, and economically with their home societies.

204.   Bogen, Elizabeth. "Ethnic Geography." Chap. 6 in *Immigration in New York*, edited by Elizabeth Bogen, 69-81. New York: Praeger, 1987. New immigrant settlement patterns are seen to be influenced by existing ethnic geography and accessible and affordable housing, as demonstrated by West

Indian settlements in Brooklyn, New York. In 1980, 56 percent of the city's West Indians lived in three Brooklyn neighborhoods. Two map figures illustrate the dramatic increase in foreign-born blacks living in Brooklyn between 1970 and 1980.

205.   Brown, Karen McCarthy. *Mama Lola: A Voudou Priestess in Brooklyn.* Berkeley: University of California Press, 1991. Explores the world of a Haitian migrant to New York City and how she adopts and modifies her family knowledge of voodoo healing and ritual in her role as a voodoo priestess. The author became a full participant, in an effort to understand voodoo as a meaningful way of life.

206.   Brown, Patricia Leigh. "Voodoo, Rooted in World Beyond, Flourishes Anew." *The New York Times* (31 December 1998): 1,5. Sect. F, Col.6. Reports on the active life of the Haitian migrant voodoo priestess Mama Lola and the religious temple created in her Brooklyn, New York basement. Other home-based temples and the history and beliefs of voodooism are also described. A new generation of Haitian Americans has come to embrace voodoo, a religion that many of their parents had rejected. Includes several relevant photographs.

207.   Buchanan, Susan H. "The Cultural Meaning of Social Class for Haitians in New York City." *Ethnic Groups* 5 (1983): 7-30. A study of the intricate Haitian social class system and the how New York City Haitians interpret their community relations in terms of sociocultural divisions that existed in Haiti. While Haitians are said to equate Brooklyn with the slums of Haiti, they equate the borough of Queens with exclusive suburbs of Port-au Prince. Social class distinctions are further maintained through social clubs and social networks.

208.   Clarke, Velta, and Veronica Udeogalanya, eds. *Adjustment of Caribbean Immigrants in New York: Social and Economic Dimensions.* New York: Caribbean Research Center, Medgar Evers College, City University of New York, 1989. Includes two papers on the adjustment of West Indian immigrants to 1980s New York City. The first work reviews some of the mechanisms used to adapt to the economic and social structure of the city. The second explores the magnitude of the migratory flow to the city and the legality of immigrant status as part of the adaptation process.

209.   Clarke, Velta J., and Emmanuel Riviere, eds. *Establishing New Lives: Selected Readings on Caribbean Immigrants in New York City.* New York: Caribbean Research Center Medgar Evers College, City University of New York, 1989. Research reports that provide a structured examination of the acculturation process of West Indian immigrants to New York City who arrived after the influx of the 1950s and 1960s. Topics covered include family structure, reunification and socialization; male/female relationships; gender and immigrant selection; maternal and child health; Jamaican nursing sector workers; housing and employment; consumer behavior; and psychological features of Jamaican immigrants.

210.   Conway, Dennis, and Ualthan Bigby. "Where Caribbean Peoples Live in New York City." Chap. 5 in *Caribbean Life in New York City: Sociocultural Dimensions*, edited by Constance R. Sutton and Elsa M. Chaney. 75-83. New York: Center for Migration Studies, Inc., 1987. Analyzes the 1980 residential patterns of Caribbean New Yorkers as reflections of cultural backgrounds, racial identity and non-assimilation with the broader society. Maps and statistical tables help illustrate the concentration of English-speaking West Indians in certain neighborhoods of Brooklyn and Queens, New York. Barbadians were the most residentially separated while Haitians lived in close proximity to English speaking Caribbean immigrants.

211.   Coombs, Orde. "West Indians in New York: Moving Beyond the Limbo Pole." *New York* 3 (1970): 28-32. Sociocultural observations of English-speaking West Indian New Yorkers, in the 1960s, who viewed America as a transitory state and embraced the values of education, hard work, home ownership, and British heritage. Assimilation into New York was aided by earlier immigrants and is contrasted with the experiences of 1930s immigrants. Descendants of 1930s immigrants were said to celebrate achievements of prominent West Indian-Americans while emphasizing their individual non-American/black heritage. Concludes that slavery's aftermath in the West Indies led to hostility to social movements emphasizing blackness.

212.   Feigelman, William, Bernard S., Gorman, et al. "The Social Characteristics of Black Catholics." *Sociology and Social Research* 75, no. 3 (1991): 133-143. National social surveys, taken between 1982 and 1987, indicated that African American Catholics were primarily foreign-born West Indians living in urban areas. Various statistical tables compare social and political characteristics of black Catholics and black Protestants.

213.   "For West Indians, Cricket Field is Bit of Home." *The New York Times* (11 July 1983): 1. Sect.B, Col.2. Cricket is seen as a cultural bonding agent for hundreds of West Indians who gather to play the game at a park in the Bronx, New York. The game serves both as a link to the homeland and as a means of adjusting to life in the United States.

214.   Jackson, Joyce M. "African American and West Indian Folklife in South Florida." *South Florida History Magazine: Quarterly of the Historical Museum of Southern Florida*, no. 3 (1990): 11-18. Includes a survey of the strategies used by West Indians in South Florida to preserve forms of their homelands' cultural practices. Strategies discussed include arts and crafts displayed in homes; musical forms enjoyed at parties and concerts; African-based storytelling; foodways reflected in ethnic restaurants and grocery stores; and the celebration of Carnival both in the home island and in Miami.

215.   Jenkins, Nancy H. "Cuisine of the Caribbean: It's Here and It's Hot; New York Embraces Island Fare." *The New York Times* (9 April 1986): 1. Sect.C, Col.6. Features an exploration of spicy Caribbean, especially Jamaican and Barbadian, food. Such food has become familiar to many New Yorkers

because of the annual West Indian Carnival, held in Brooklyn. Describes a major food market area in East Harlem and one in Brooklyn that specializes in West Indian fruits, vegetables, meat, fish, and spices.

216.   Klockenbrink, Myra. "If You're thinking of Living in: Crown Heights." *The New York Times* (20 January 1985): 9. Sect.8, Col.1. A real-estate assessment of the Crown Heights neighborhood of Brooklyn, New York that is populated by Asians, Native American blacks, West Indians, Haitians, and Lubavitch sect Jews.

217.   Marshall, Paule. "Rising Islanders of Bed-Stuy." *The New York Times* (3 November 1985): 67. Sect.6, Pt.2, Col.2. Brooklyn's Bedford-Stuyvesant neighborhood is seen as an area that reflects Caribbean society with outdoor food stands and bakeries selling Caribbean goods. The neighborhood expanded with new waves of Caribbean immigrants since the 1960s. Population statistics (total and percentage) are also given for West Indians for the 1960s and 1970s. Inter-relationships with native born blacks are also addressed.

218.   Morgan, Thomas. "Caribbean Verve Brightens New York." *The New York Times* (3 June 1988): 1. Sect.B, Col.2. The value of Caribbean self-help organizations in Brooklyn, New York is discussed in relation to New York City's attraction to these immigrants. Notes that some 800,000 Caribbean immigrants have settled in New York City since 1980.

219.   "Profile: Antoine Adrien." *Migration Today* 7, no. 4 (1979): 45-46. Profiles a Haitian Roman Catholic priest working with the Brooklyn, New York Haitian community in the 1970s. This overwhelming young and needy population looked to Adrien for leadership and guidance. Illiteracy and superstition also characterized this largely undocumented population. Includes a list of Haitian American community organizations operating in the metropolitan area in the 1970s.

220.   Sandis, Eva. "Some Sociological Observations on Voluntary Organizations among Recent Immigrants in New York." *Journal of Voluntary Action Research* 6 (1977): 98-101. Compares contemporary studies of recent and earlier West Indian and Chinese immigrants to urban areas, including New York City. Maintains that many post-1965 immigrants are professionals who form social networks, which tend to exclude their non-professional fellow immigrant nationals.

221.   Thomas, Bert J. "Caribbean-American Associations: Activism or Parochialism?" *TransAfrica Forum* 5, no. 3 (1988): 45-59. Reports on 1982-1986 studies of New York City area West Indian voluntary organizations. Most were apolitical and concentrated on social events and fundraising for causes in home societies. These associations also emphasized class distinctions and the desire for respectability, precluding radical political mobilization. Comparisons between such organizations in early 20th century Harlem and the 1980s reveal the effect of individualism and the Caribbean personality.

222. Thomas, Bert J. "Historical Functions of Caribbean-American Benevolent/Progressive Associations." *Afro-Americans in New York Life and History* 12 (1988): 45-58. Outlines the role of Caribbean mutual aid societies in helping West Indian immigrants find housing, employment, and medical care in New York City. Also discussed is the role these societies play in aiding these immigrants to assimilate to American culture while retaining their Caribbean ethnicity.

223. Tobias, Peter M. "Differential Adaptation of Grenadian Emigrant Communities in London and New York." *Social and Economic Studies* 25 (1976): 77-80. An anthropologist discusses his work and that of another scholar's by comparing the social-economic adaptation of Grenadians in London vs. those in New York City. Social relations such as frequenting bars/pubs, marriage practices, and helping behaviors such as mutual aid societies are discussed. Grenadians are said to experience an environmentally different social situation in New York than in London.

224. Toney, Joyce Roberta. "The Development of a Culture of Migration Among a Caribbean People: St. Vincent and New York, 1838-1979." Ph.D. Dissertation, Columbia University (New York City), 1986. A cultural study of immigrants from St. Vincent to New York City, from 1838 to 1979. These immigrants continued to strongly identify with the sending society in an effort to avoid accepting the perceived lower social status of indigenous African Americans.

225. Trabold, Robert A. "Neighborhood Immigrant Popular Religion: A New Interpretation." Ph.D. Dissertation, City University of New York, 1988. A Roman Catholic street festival is seen as a symbol of Caribbean popular culture and religion among immigrants in the East Flatbush neighborhood of Brooklyn, New York. These belief systems are said to conflict with American industrial culture and the goals of the Second Vatican Council. However, seeds of political and social liberation are found in this popular immigrant culture.

226. Trabold, Robert. "Pastoral Strategies in the Immigrant Work." *Migration Today* 9, no. 4-5 (1981): 40-48. Describes the role of an immigrant parish church, in Brooklyn, New York, which worked to aid the acculturation process of Caribbean immigrants after World War II and Haitian immigrants starting in 1968.

227. Wenski, Thomas G. "The New Immigrants: Tensions and Opportunities for the Church in America." *Migration World Magazine* 26, no. 4 (1998): 33-36. The American Roman Catholic Church is seen as middle-class and suburban and therefore invisible to less fortunate Haitian immigrants. The establishment of Haitian national parish structures is said to give poorer immigrants a stake in the church and the society. Declares that successful evangelism is enculturation.

CRIME

228.   Barton, D. "Kansas City Experience: 'Crack' Organized Crime Cooperative Task Force." *The Police Chief* 55 (1988): 28, 30-31. Experiences of the Kansas City, Missouri Police Department, between 1985 and 1987, "illustrate the impact of Jamaican/Caribbean basin organized crime on drug-related crime" throughout the United States. A special task force found "that Jamaicans were being transported for the sole purpose of distributing ['crack'] cocaine."

229.   Colwell, J. G. A. "Caribbeans in U.S. Prisons." *Everybody's: The Caribbean-American Magazine* 21, no. 8 (31 October 1997): 13-14. Reports on the number of Jamaican nationals being held in the American federal and New York State penal systems. Describes the American justice system as being prejudiced against Jamaicans, often denying them due process and supportive counsel. Expresses hope for the passage of a proposed prisoner transfer treaty with Jamaica.

230.   Hamid, Ansley. "From Ganja to Crack: Caribbean Participation in the Underground Economy in Brooklyn, 1976-1986. Part 1. Establishment of the Marijuana Economy." *The International Journal of the Addictions* 26, no. 6 (1991): 615-628. Describes the participation of Caribbean youth in various drug distribution networks, from the mid-1960s to 1987, throughout the Caribbean region and in North America. Explores relationships between the underground drug economy and the mainstream capitalist economy. Many who succeeded in the marijuana networks, of the 1970s reinvested revenues in cottage industry and agriculture in the Caribbean.

231.   Hamid, Ansley. "From Ganja to Crack: Caribbean Participation in the Underground Economy in Brooklyn, 1976-1986. Part 2. Establishment of the Cocaine (and Crack) Economy." *The International Journal of the Addictions* 26, no. 7 (1991): 729-738. Profiles four Rastafarian marijuana dealers based in Brooklyn, New York. Increased police attacks on marijuana in New York and the Caribbean led to a recession in the dealers' business. These dealers switched to distributing and using cocaine despite Rastafarian taboos. Personal use of cocaine proved ruinous to the dealers' networks of distribution. The Brooklyn drug economy was transformed and low level distributors became very transitory.

232.   Hamid, Ansley. "The Political Economy of Crack-Related Violence." *Contemporary Drug Problems* 17, no. 1 (1990): 31-78. Chronicles the socioeconomic status of drug users and sellers through a history of the changes in the political/economic structure of a Brooklyn, New York West Indian neighborhood over 25 years. Also studies the political economy of "crack" (cocaine) related violence.

233.   Kail, Barbara L., and Paula H. Kleinman. "Fear, Crime, Community Organization, and Limitations on Daily Routines." *Urban Affairs Quarterly* 20

(1985): 400-408. Working on the assumption that West Indians have stronger formal community organizations than whites or native blacks, the authors examine five hypotheses concerning these groups' relative fear of crime. Statistical sampling techniques, used in two Brooklyn, New York neighborhoods, bore out some of the hypotheses but not others.

234.   Quimby, Ernest. "Drug Trafficking and the Caribbean Connection: Survival Mechanisms, Entrepreneurship, and Social Symptoms." *Urban League Review* 14 (1990): 61-70. Sociopolitical and ethnographic analyses of drug trafficking among West Indians in Brooklyn, New York. Emphasizes the Jamaican drug culture.

235.   "Rasta Crime: A Confidential Report by the N.Y.C. P.D." *Caribbean Review* 14 (1985): 12-15. Reprints an excerpt from a confidential 1983 New York City Police Department report on crime among Jamaican Rastafarians.

236.   Seamonds, Jack, et al. "Ethnic Gangs and Organized Crime." *U.S. News & World Report* 104 (18 January 1988): 29-34. Reports on the growth of gangs and organized crime, among Asian and West Indian immigrants, in the United States in the 1980s. Considers the violence of Jamaican criminals and the evolution of their gangs, called posses (pronounced passes), which thrived on illegal drug dealing and gunrunning.

237.   Smith, Abe. "Jamaican Youth Flee U.S. Sex and Drugs Trap: Teenage Immigrants are Being Sent Home to Escape the Dark Side of the American Dream." *The Weekly Journal* 175 (7 September 1995): 8-9. Discusses the trend of Jamaican immigrant teenagers being sent back to Jamaica after succumbing to truancy, drug abuse, crime, and sexual abuse in the United States and Canada. Reports on Jamaican rehabilitation efforts to aid the returnees.

238.   Tanton, J., and W. Lutton. "Immigration and Criminality in the U.S.A." *The Journal of Social, Political and Economic Studies* 18 (1993): 217-234. Documents a major increase in the incarceration rate for aliens in the United States and maintains that international crime and terrorist organizations view the United States as fertile territory. Documents the criminal activities of various nationalities including Jamaicans, who specialize in cocaine.

239.   Warshaw, Bob, and Paul Daly. "Drug Trafficking in the United States." *The Police Chief* 63 (1996): 18-19, 21-23. Describes the violence connected with the spread of crack cocaine in the United States. Those directly involved in the distribution and use include certain gangs of Dominicans and Jamaicans.

240.   Witkin, Gordon. "The Men Who Created Crack." *U.S. News & World Report* (19 August 1991): 44-53. Banking on the profit potential of the narcotic "crack" cocaine, Jamaican traffickers are said to have focussed initially on the large Caribbean populations of New York City and Miami, Florida in the mid-1980s.

CULTURAL ACTIVITIES

241.   Allen, Ray, and Lois Wilcken, eds. *Island Sounds in the Global City: Caribbean Music and Identity in New York*. New York: New York Folklore Society and The Institute for Studies in American Music, Brooklyn College, City University of New York, 1998. Essays that survey popular musical styles from the West Indies and the Hispanic Caribbean and the relationship between this music and cultural identity in New York City. Caribbean music reflects an ongoing cultural exchange in a city seen as a transnational crossroads. Popular Haitian music, Trinidadian calypso and steel pan music, and Jamaican reggae not only define ethnic groups but also help negotiate relations between groups.

242.   Barber, Beverly A. "Pearl Primus, In Search of Her Roots: 1943-1970." Ph.D. Dissertation, Florida State University (Tallahassee), 1984. A Biographical study of Pearl Primus, dancer and choreographer, who migrated from Trinidad to New York City at an early age. Views her work in terms of the sociopolitical conditions of the 1940s, its impact in chronicling the black American experience, and traditional dances of Africa and the Caribbean.

243.   Buchanan, Susan H. "Haitians in the Arts." *Migration Today* 7, no. 4 (1979): 33-38. A photographic essay that sees Haitian painting, dance and music in New York City as maintaining links to traditional Haitian culture while pursuing new meaning and content.

244.   Carlson, Alvar W. "A Geographical Analysis of America's Ethnic Radio Programming." *The Social Science Journal* 34, no. 3 (1997): 285-295. This analysis "reveals the persistence of [radio] programs for certain ethnic populations and the emergence of new programs that are associated with America's changing ethnic diversity due to the growth in immigration from Asia and Latin America, including the Caribbean."

245.   Cooper, Wayne F. "Stranger and Pilgrim: The Life of Claude McKay, 1890-1948." Ph.D. Dissertation, Rutgers The State University of New Jersey (New Brunswick), 1982. A comprehensive biography of Claude McKay, the Jamaican-American author, who lived in New York City, Jamaica, Europe, and North Africa during his lifetime. He sought to comment on major sociopolitical events of his time and his poetry and fiction gave expression to the peasant and black working class cultures of the West Indies and the United States.

246.   Glick-Schiller, Nina, and Georges Fouron. "Everywhere We Go, We Are in Danger: Ti Manno and the Emergence of a Haitian Transnational Identity." *American Ethnologist* 17, no. 2 (1990): 329-347. Examines the lyrics of a Haitian immigrant singer who was popular in New York City during the 1970s and early 1980s. The Haitian immigrants' responses to this singer's message helps to interpret factors of class, race, ethnicity, and nationalism that shape Haitian-American identities. Ti Manno conveyed a sense of community that was used by Haitian leaders.

247.   Hathaway, Heather A. "Cultural Crossings: Migration, Generation, and Gender in Writings by Claude McKay and Paule Marshall." Ph.D. Dissertation, Harvard University (Cambridge, Mass.), 1993. "...Examines the literary and cultural impact of African Caribbean immigration to America by analyzing the themes of migration, generation, and gender in the writings of two of the most prominent black immigrant authors in the United States." Specifically, the study explores the parameters of the black migration narrative and the impact of African Caribbean writers on black American letters.

248.   Heim, Chris. "Rap 'n' Reggae: Shinehead Pushes the Boundaries of Streetwise Music from the South Bronx All the Way to His Native Jamaica." *Chicago Tribune* (9 February 1989): 13A. Sect. 5, Col.1. Disc Jockeys and emcees are described as the catalysts in the birth of rap music from the roots of Jamaican reggae. The work of these disc jockeys and West Indian immigrants to New York City thus transformed reggae into rap music.

249.   Huggins, Winston G. "A Critical Study of Six Jamaican Artists in the Context of an Emerging Caribbean Culture in New York: An Aesthetic Inquiry." Ph.D. Dissertation, New York University (New York City), 1993. Examines the work of six Jamaican New York artists in an effort to determine the extent to which their work is reflective of Jamaican culture and of the experiences of these artists in New York City.

250.   LeSeur, Geta. "One Mother, Two Daughters: The Afro-American and The Afro-Caribbean Female Bildungsroman." *New Jersey History* 17, no. 2 (1986): 26-33. LeSeur compares the treatment of involuntary migration from Africa to plantations in the West Indies and the United States in fiction describing young girls' lives, as seen in the novels of immigrant African Caribbean and African American writers.

251.   Nelson, Emmanuel S. "Black America and the Anglophone Afro Caribbean Literary Consciousness." *Amerikastudien/American Studies* [Germany] 12, no. 4 (1989): 53-58. "Discusses the varying influences of revolutionary black American literature on three English-speaking Caribbean immigrant writers" whose work reflects experiences of blacks in the African Diaspora. The writers explored are Edward Brathwaite, Derek Walcott, and Paule Marshall.

252.   Stange, Maren. "Shadow and Substance." *Art in America* 84 (March) (1996): 35-39. Profiles the prolific career of Guggenheim award-winning photographer, Roy DeCarava, born to Jamaican parents in Harlem, in 1919. "One of the first African American photographers to gain prominence and depict black life," his career is chronicled up to 1989. Includes a bibliography of publications that reproduce his work.

253.   Stevenson, Peggy L. "Conflicts of Culture, Class and Gender in Selected Caribbean-American and Caribbean Women's Literature." Ph.D. Dissertation, Howard University (Washington, D.C.), 1989. Studies the themes of conflict in culture, class and gender in the fictional writings of three

Caribbean female authors. Chapter one examines the problems of West Indian assimilation in American and European society as examined in the novels of Rosa Guy and Paule Marshall. Chapter two examines problems of class conflict in the works of Guy, Marshall, Zee Edgell, and Merle Hodge. Chapter three examines gender conflict in the works of Guy and Marshall.

254.   Trabold, Robert. "A Festive Caribbean Immigrant Community in New York City: A Self-Image." *Migration World Magazine* 18, no. 1 (1990): 18-23. Participants in a festive Caribbean religious procession were interviewed, in order to discover their adjustment to life in New York City in the face of its great contrast to life in the Caribbean. The cooperative efforts of the festival created unity in the face of problems these Caribbean immigrants faced.

255.   Twining, Mary. "The Flower in the Boat: Folk Art of the Migrant Workers of Mid-New York State." *New York Folklore* 13, no. 1/2 (1987): 49-57. Studies the significance of plants and boats and folk art in the lives of West Indian and other migrant farm workers in New York State.

256.   Wilcken, Lois Eileen. "Music Folklore among Haitians in New York: Staged Representations and the Negotiation of Identity." Ph.D. Dissertation, Columbia University, 1991. A study of the relationship between Haitian immigrants' self-identification and their interest in Haitian folkloric musical productions in New York. Productions heavily imbued with African culture, the study finds, receive minimal support from Haitian immigrants in New York City. Class divisions in Haiti, strong neo-colonial influences there, and the American media's negative approach to Haiti's African culture are said to prevent Haitian immigrants from identifying with their African heritage.

WEST INDIAN AMERICAN DAY CARNIVAL

257.   Buff, Rachel J. "Calling Home: Migration, Race, and Popular Memory in Caribbean Brooklyn and Native-American Minneapolis, 1945-1992." Ph.D. Dissertation, University of Minnesota, 1995. A study of two festivals: West Indian-American Day Carnival in Brooklyn, New York and urban Indian powwows in Minneapolis, Minnesota." "The study focuses on the emergence of collective cultural identities among Caribbean immigrants and Native American migrants to these cities" since World War II.

258.   Bumiller, Elisabeth. "Unwinding to a Caribbean Rhythm." *The New York Times* (8 September 1998): 3+. Sect.B, Col.1, Metropolitan Desk. Describes the activities surrounding the 31st annual West Indian American Day Carnival, which took place in Brooklyn, New York. Details local Carnival-related selling activities and the participation of New York City's mayor and candidates for his office. Includes photos of costumed participants.

259.   Dao, James. "A Caribbean Party; Crown Heights Parade Spreads Joy." *The New York Times* (8 September 1992): 3. Sect.B, Col.1. Reports on the 25th annual West Indian Day Parade in Brooklyn, New York. The Parade is seen to be a reflection of the growing significance of the region's West Indian population.

260.   Hill, Donald R., and Robert Abramson. "West Indian Carnival in Brooklyn." *Natural History* 88 (August) (1979): 72-85. Describes Brooklyn, New York's West Indian Carnival, as one of the nation's largest folk festivals. Brooklyn's mid-1970s West Indian population reinforces its identity as West Indian through this celebration. The history of the Carnival is traced to West Indian festivals of planters and slaves, to Harlem during the period of the 1920s to 1964, and finally to Brooklyn where the Carnival was re-established in 1969. Calypso music, steel bands and "mas" (masquerade) bands are explored as the most obvious elements of the festivities.

261.   Jones, Charisse. "West Indian Parade Returns to Fill Streets of Brooklyn." *The New York Times* (1 September 1996): 41+. Sect.1, Col.4. Reports on preparations for Brooklyn's annual West Indian Carnival and parade held on Labor Day. Back lots in Flatbush Brooklyn become festive courtyards and garages and backyards become sewing factories for participants' costumes. The carnival's historical background is explained. Weekend activities include masqueraders competing for prizes, a reggae concert, a children's' carnival, and the battle of Calypsonians. Includes photos of prepared costumes and children practicing their dance steps.

262.   Kasinitz, Philip, and Judith Freidenberg-Herbstein. "The Puerto Rican Parade and West Indian Carnival: Public Celebrations in New York City." in *Caribbean Life in New York City: Sociocultural Dimensions*, edited by Constance R. Sutton and Elsa M. Chaney, 327-349. New York, New York: Center for Migration Studies of New York, Inc., 1987. Compares these two ethnic celebrations and their political significance. The clear sense of nationhood, symbolized in the Puerto Rican parade, is compared to a sense of ethnic uniqueness, symbolized by the West Indian celebration. Other contrasts deals with parade organizational structure, leadership strengths and weaknesses and inclusion versus exclusion seen in the West Indian Carnival.

263.   Kennedy, Randy. "At 30, Caribbean Festival Is Bursting at Seams." *The New York Times* (2 September 1997): 3+. Sect.B, Col. 1. Describes the activities of various Caribbean tourists who have come to New York for the annual West Indian American Day Carnival parade. Preparations for the parade begin weeks before and celebrators gather at their respective camps for all-night preparations and rogue parades.

264.   Kifner, John. "In Brooklyn, Steel Drums and a Truce." *The New York Times* (3 September 1991): 1. Sect.B, Col.2. Reports on the annual West Indian Day Carnival parade, which took place following two weeks of tension and

violence between blacks and Hasidic Jews. Many Hasidim attended the Carnival parade as spectators.

265.   Manning, Frank E. "Overseas Caribbean Carnivals: The Art and Politics of a Transnational Celebration." *Plantation Society in the Americas* 3, no. 1 (1990): 47-62. Studies the effect of the Caribbean migratory flow on the establishment of new carnival traditions in North America and Britain. Contrasts the West Indian carnivals held in Toronto, Brooklyn, and London. Sees carnival as an attempt to retain cultural identity.

266.   Nagourney, Adam. "Parade Is Stumping Ground for Mayoral Candidates." *The New York Times* (2 September 1997): 1+. Sect.B, Col.2. New York City's Mayor and three mayoral candidates join celebrants in the annual West Indian American Day parade. The mayor and his challengers received differing receptions from the onlookers. Various candidates took the opportunity to comment on a recent case of police abuse of a Haitian immigrant.

267.   Ojito, Mirta. "Brooklyn Goes Caribbean on West Indian-American Day." *The New York Times* (3 September 1996): 3+. Sect.B, Col.1. Describes the participation of several recent West Indian immigrants in the annual West Indian Carnival in Brooklyn, New York. The activities of an immigrant photographer and hundreds of vendors are also detailed. Includes a photograph of a 6-year-old parade participant.

268.   Pareles, Jon. "It's Carnival Time as New York Turns Caribbean to Dance the Weekend Away." *The New York Times* (31 August 1990): 1. Sect.C, Col.1. The West African roots of the music featured during New York City's West Indian Day Carnival and parade are discussed. Costumes plus West Indian food and drink are also discussed as major aspects of the multi-day festival, which culminates in an elaborate parade.

269.   Pareles, Jon. "New York's Carnival, All Grown Up." *The New York Times* (31 August 1990): 19. Sect.C, Col.2. Reviews the development of New York City's two carnivals based on African culture. These were the West Indian Carnival in Brooklyn and the Pan-American Carnival in Manhattan. Both take place on Labor Day weekend.

270.   Pierre-Pierre, Garry. "Success of West Indian Parade Brings Dissension." *The New York Times* (17 June 1998): Sect.B, Pg. 8, Col.1. Reports on challenges to the leaders of Brooklyn, New York's West Indian Day Carnival parade by many of the parade's bandleaders. Bandleaders' charge that the large parade is becoming unmanageable for the organizers and the bandleaders would like to share in money raised from corporate parade sponsors.

271.   Purdy, Matthew. "Parade Shows Off West Indian Political Clout." *The New York Times* (6 September 1994): 1. Sect.A. The presence of New York State's Governor, New York City's Mayor and various other political figures at the 1994 West Indian Day Carnival parade, emphasized the growing political

significance of this event and of the Caribbean community. Caribbean culture was displayed in food, floats and costumes but political culture was just as evident with campaign signs on street light poles.

272.   Sengupta, Somini, and Garry Pierre-Pierre. "A Tradition Remade in Brooklyn; West Indians Prepare a Lavish, and Popular Pageant." *The New York Times* (5 September 1998): 1+. Sect.B, Col.2. Reports on outdoor orchestra rehearsals for the upcoming West Indian Day Carnival and parade. The carnival reflects both increased Caribbean immigration and immigrants' newly found interest in carnival as a cultural icon. Discusses dissention between parade organizers and some bandleaders. Explains that the parade has also fueled the resurgence of another Trinidadian rite, J'ouvert.

273.   Smith, Michael P. "New Orleans' Carnival Culture from the Underside." *Plantation Society in the Americas* 3, no. 1 (1990): 11-32. Finds that the American carnival tradition is rooted in the Creole traditions of black communities of the Caribbean and the American South. Details how blacks in New Orleans have attempted to maintain Mardi Gras customs that are separate from those of whites. The resultant parades, of the black community include unique costumes and music. This New Orleans' Carnival, therefore, shares some of the same traditions of Brooklyn, New York's annual West Indian Carnival.

274.   Tabor, Mary. "The Lilting Sound and Soul of Immigration." *The New York Times* (6 September 1992): 51. Sect.1, Col.1. Notes that the Labor Day weekend Carnival and parade in Brooklyn, New York is second only to Trinidad's Carnival in importance for West Indians. The history of the New York event is traced from its 1940s beginnings in Harlem. West Indians are said to constitute some 50% of the annual foreign migratory flow to New York City in the early 1990s.

275.   Van Capelleveen, Remco. "The Caribbeanization of New York City: West Indian Festival in Brooklyn." *Revue Francaise d'Etudes Americaines* [France] 17, no. 51 (1992): 27-34. Sees the massive annual West Indian American festival, in Brooklyn, as a symbol of increased African-Caribbean immigration. This influx is said to have caused the "Caribbeanization" of parts of New York City and thus the cultural, social, political, and economic separation of these communities from the rest of the city.

276.   Yarrow, Andrew L. "In Brooklyn, Harkening to the Steel-Drum Beat." *The New York Times* (3 September 1990): 25. Sect.A, Col.1. Explores the significance of music and steel drums in the annual West Indian Day Carnival parade, held in Brooklyn, New York. Also traces the history of steel drums from Trinidad, the origins of the parade and the making of parade costumes. Includes a photograph of steel drummers practicing for the parade.

Chapter 3

Economic Life

GENERAL STUDIES

301.   "Black Like Me: Race in America." *The Economist* 339 (11 May) (1996): 27-28. Investigates factors that cause immigrants from the Caribbean and Africa to often enjoy a higher standard of living than native-born blacks. One reason explored is the higher percentage of two-parent, two-income families among these immigrant groups. Evidence also indicates more entrepreneurial skills among black immigrants than native-born blacks.

302.   Blauner, Peter. "Islands in the City (Brooklyn West Indians)." *New York* 19 (21 April) (1986): 66-73. The success of individual immigrants from Guyana and Trinidad illustrates the role that many West Indians have played in the revitalization of such Brooklyn, New York, neighborhoods as East Flatbush and Crown Heights. Roles as homeowners, landlords, entrepreneurs, and political activists illustrate much of this success. However, political impact has been slowed by conflicts within the West Indian community and with native-born blacks.

303.   Bonnett, Aubrey W. "An Examination of Rotating Credit Associations among Black West Indian Immigrants in Brooklyn." In *Sourcebook on the New Immigration: Implications for the United States and the International Community*, edited by Roy S. Bryce-Laporte, 271-283. New Brunswick, N.J.: Transaction Books, 1980. Examines the 1970s' use of rotating credit associations among English-speaking West Indians, including Guyanese, in Brooklyn, New York. Related Caribbean traditions are explored in terms of slavery and the differing regional names for such organizations. Current usage indicates generational differences and parental influence on credit association use. Also explored are the effects of credit associations' organizational structure and adaptive functions on their members.

304.   Bonnett, Aubrey W. *Institutional Adaptation of West Indian Immigrants to America: An analysis of Rotating Credit Associations*. Washington, D.C.: University Press of America, 1981. A general study of rotating credit asso-

ciations, which emphasizes their significance among the West Indian community in Brooklyn, New York. Organization and practices, generational usage, overlap with the commercial banking and credit systems, and the social adaptive functions of these associations, are among the topics explored.

305.   Bonnett, Aubrey W. "Structured Adaptation of Black Migrants from the Caribbean: An Examination of an Indigenous Banking System in Brooklyn." *Phylon* 42 (1981): 346-355. Transplanted from the Caribbean to Brooklyn, rotating credit associations create loan funds that are available to regular contributors "in rotation." Organizational structure, typical size, contributions, and order of rotation are among the factors explored for these generational adaptive entities. The similarity and relationships between these associations and the traditional banking system is another major theme covered.

306.   Bonnett, Aubrey W. "West Indians in the United States of America: Some Theoretical and Practical Considerations." Chap. 6 in *Emerging Perspectives on the Black Diaspora*, edited by Aubrey W. Bonnett and G. Llewellyn Watson, 149-163. Lanham, Maryland: University Press of America, 1990. The perceived success of West Indians vs. native African Americans is considered an idealistic concept due to varied ethnic adaptations of West Indians, responding to America's racial climate. Some seek links with native blacks, others pursue ethnic "altercasting" for social mobility, while others are relegated to an ethnic underclass.

307.   Boswell, Thomas D. "In the Eye of the Storm: The Context of Haitian Migration to Miami, Florida." *Southeastern Geographer* 23, no. 2 (November) (1983): 57-77.   Haitian migrants to South Florida have increased visibility because of their overall poverty, their race, their population concentration, and their often-illegal alien status. Haitians who migrated to New York are compared to those who migrated to South Florida.

308.   Bryce-Laporte, Roy S. "New York City and the New Caribbean Immigration: A Contextual Statement." Chap. 4 in *Caribbean Life in New York City: Sociocultural Dimensions*, edited by Constance R. Sutton and Elsa M. Chaney, 54-73. New York: Center for Migration Studies, 1987. The 1960-70 flow of West Indian immigrants to New York City was affected by the city's role as the financial center of a system in which the Caribbean became increasingly dependent. In New York City, immigrants faced an economy changed by the 1970s fiscal crisis that resulted in increased ethnic antagonism. Identified as part of the native black minority, West Indians faced intense antagonisms of race, ethnicity, and class. Reactions to antagonism and the co-mingling of many Caribbean nationalities, helped create a Pan-Caribbean consciousness.

309.   Butcher, Kristin F. "Black Immigrants in the United States: A Comparison with Native Blacks and Other Immigrants." *Industrial and Labor Relations Review* 47, no. 2 (1994): 265-284. This statistical analysis of 1980 United States Census data indicates higher rates of employment in 1979 for immigrant black men than for native-born American black men. However,

wages for employed members of both groups were equivalent and existing wage differences stemmed primarily from the immigration selection process. Among the statistical information included are annual earnings and educational achievement for black and Latino-Caribbean immigrant men.

310. Chiswick, Barry R. "Immigrants in the U.S. Labor Market." *Annals of the American Academy of Political and Social Science* 460 (March) (1982): 64-72. Surveys the increase in immigration to the United States from Asia, Latin America, and the West Indies. Finds that adult male immigrants have comparable earnings to the native-born. However, differences among the immigrants are due to amount of time in the United States, reason for migrating, and country of origin.

311. D'Amico, Thomas F. "The Economics of Market and Nonmarket Racial Discrimination." Ph.D. Dissertation, New York University (New York City), 1983. Investigates the importance of labor market vs. non-labor-market discrimination as determinants for the relatively low earnings of blacks in the United States. Examining 1970 census data, West Indian blacks were used as a control group to explore the theory that, as immigrants, they were not subject to non-market discrimination. Comparisons of West-Indian-to-white and West-Indian-to-native-black earnings indicated the power of strong and growing labor market and non-labor market discrimination.

312. Daneshvary, Nasser. "Black Immigrants in the U.S. Labor Market: An Earnings Analysis." *The Review of Black Political Economy* 22, no. 3 (Winter) (1994): 77-98. Employing the Public Use Sample of the 1980 census, "this article investigates the existence and sources of earnings differences between black Americans and black immigrants, and between black and nonblack immigrants." The major regions of origin of black immigrants are identified as Africa, Central America, and South America.

313. DeFreitas, Gregory E. "What is the Occupational Mobility of Black Immigrants." *Monthly Labor Review* 104 (April) (1981): 44-45. An examination of the occupational mobility of black immigrants to the New York City/New Jersey area "through comparisons with their pre-migration occupations and with the occupational mobility of native-born blacks." Finds that the black immigrants were more likely to experience downward occupational mobility than native-born blacks and whites.

314. Dodoo, F[rancis] Nil-Amoo. "Assimilation Differences Among Africans in America." *Social Forces* 76 (1997): 527-546. An examination of the "hourly earnings of [male] African Americans, Caribbean immigrants, and Africans in the United States," based on the 1990 Census. While Caribbean immigrants outearn the other two groups, the study finds Africans are poorly rewarded for their higher education obtained abroad. This leads to a conclusion that the earnings advantages of Caribbean immigrants may be primarily due to "differential acceptance by American society."

315.   Dodoo, F[rancis] Nil-Amoo. "Blacks and Earnings in New York State." *Sociological Spectrum* 11, no. 2 (1991): 203-212. Based on 1980 Census data, earnings of Jamaican immigrants to New York City are demonstrated to be less than indigenous African Americans both in that city and nationwide. The role of discrimination is found to be less significant in New York than nationwide. As the role of discrimination is less than nationwide, New York State is a rational economic choice as a destination for Jamaican immigrants.

316.   Dodoo, F[rancis] Nil-Amoo. "Earnings Differences Among Blacks in America." *Social Science Research* 20, no. 2 (1991): 93-108. Explores the reasons that native black males had 5% higher earnings than foreign black males, as of the 1980 United States Census. This was so even though foreign blacks had a higher average level of schooling than native blacks. Statistically determines that if foreign blacks were rewarded at rates identical to native blacks, immigrant black earnings would surpass those of native blacks. This finding is described as the "cost" of foreign birth.

317.   Dodoo, F[rancis] Nil-Amoo. "Minority Immigrants in the United States: Earnings Attributes and Economic Success." *Canadian Studies in Population* 18, no. 2 (1991): 42-55. "Data from the 1980 Census...are used to explore variances in earnings attainment among male immigrants from Jamaica, Mexico and China." While Chinese immigrants had the highest hourly wages, these were found to result primarily from substantial differences in labor market characteristics. Some of these characteristics included occupation, experience, and time of migration.

318.   Dodoo, Francis [Nil-Amoo]. "Race and Immigrant Stratification in the United States." Ph.D. Dissertation, University of Pennsylvania (Philadelphia), 1988. Investigates the process of determining earnings by black immigrants to the United States in an attempt to explain differences in earnings between these immigrants and indigenous blacks. United States Census data from 1980 are used to statistically analyze differences in earnings. Finds that earnings differentials are due primarily to racial discrimination and not immigrant status.

319.   Dunn, Marvin. *Black Miami in the Twentieth Century*. Gainesville: University of Florida Press, 1997. Explores the "history of African Americans in South Florida and their pivotal role in the growth and development of Miami." An assessment of the community in the late 1990s includes the consideration of the effect of recent waves of immigration from Latin American and the Caribbean. Includes material on Marcus Garvey's Back-to-Africa movement in Miami and the socio-economic role of Bahamians and Haitians in the city.

320.   Foner, Nancy. "West Indians in New York City and London: A Comparative Analysis." *International Migration Review* 13, no. 2 (1979): 284-297. Three factors are explored as possible causes for the fact that West Indians in the United States are more successful occupationally than those in Great Britain.

This comparative occupational success may also explain why West Indians in New York City have a higher degree of occupational success than native black New Yorkers.

321.   Forsythe, Dennis. "Black Immigrants and the American Ethos: Theories and Observations." In *Caribbean Immigration to the United States: RIIES Occasional Papers No. 1*, edited by Roy S. Bryce-Laporte and Delores M. Mortimer, 55-82. Washington, D.C.: Smithsonian Institution, 1983. ERIC, ED 283 890. Argues that the most unifying aspect of America is its common capitalistic culture that offers unequal economic opportunities. West Indian immigrants' backgrounds and their migration experiences give them a "Protestant spirit," enabling them to benefit from America's economic system. Various measures are used to demonstrate West Indians' economic success in the United States since the early 20th century.

322.   Frankel, Bruce. "New York Haitians Proud: We Try Hard." *USA Today* (15 July 1993): 8. Sect.A, Col.3. Many Haitian immigrants to New York City are said to succeed well economically, with recent arrivals earning a few thousand dollars less annually than the average for the city's households.

323.   Gans, Herbert J. "Second-Generation Decline: Scenarios for the Economic and Ethnic Futures of the Post-1965 American Immigrants." *Ethnic and Racial Studies* 15, no. 2 (1992): 173-192. Hypothesizes that West Indian and other second-generation descendants of post 1965 immigrants to the United States might face poverty because of a reluctance to accept immigrant wages and working conditions. Suggests that technical and professional education might be a more effective means of upward mobility than for earlier immigrant groups.

324.   Gerlus, Jean-Claude. "The Political Economy of Haitian Migration: A Cross-Frontier Study of the Circulation of People, Capital, and Commodity Flows." Ph.D. Dissertation, State University of New York at Binghamton, 1992. Explores the economic integration of the Caribbean region into the United States in the early 20th century. In the process Haiti became a supplier a labor first to United States firms in the Caribbean and then through encouraged migration to the United States from 1915 to 1934. Due to Haitian economic policies, the 1970s brought further migration that was transformed into self-perpetuating migration networks.

325.   Glantz, Oscar. "Locus of Control and Aspiration to Traditionally Open and Traditionally Closed Occupations." *The Journal of Negro Education* 46, no. 3 (1977): 278-290. A 1971 study comparing West Indian and African American college students on the relationship of an individual's perceived internal ability, versus the significance of outside forces, to determine personal outcome as a predictor of occupational choice. Sense-of-control over one's environment was found to be a neutral factor for West Indians causing them to aspire more often to traditionally closed careers. Includes a table comparing indicators of

socioeconomic class among these two groups and their aspiration to various career categories.

326.   Grasmuck, Sherri, and Ramon Grosfoguel. "Geopolitics, Economic Niches, and Gendered Social Capital among Recent Caribbean Immigrants in New York." *Sociological Perspectives* 40, no. 3 (1997): 339-363. Examines the different socio-economic outcomes of immigrant groups from the Dominican Republic, Haiti, Cuba, Jamaica, and Puerto Rico to New York City in the last half of the twentieth century. Maintains that the differing fates of these groups require consideration of structural variables such as gender dynamics and women's labor force participation.

327.   Gupta, Udayan. "From Other Shores." *Black Enterprise* 13, no. 8 (1983): 51-54. Explores the fears of indigenous black Americans that Asian, Hispanic and Caribbean immigrants are socioeconomically displacing black Americans. Reports that many immigrants arrive with better skills than indigenous Americans have and that those with lesser skills often accept horrendous working conditions. Finds little evidence that indigenous blacks have been displaced economically.

328.   Hall, Herman. "Dr. Benjamin Watkins and the West Indian Community of New York City." *Everybody's: The Caribbean-American Magazine* 20 (31 March 1996): 23-28. A biographical sketch of Dr. Benjamin W. Watkins who was born in Barbados and later became a leader in the black community of Harlem and other areas of New York City. He was a major owner of the Inner-City Broadcasting Corporation and a board member of Carver Federal Savings Bank, with successful branches in West Indian neighborhoods.

329.   Herradas-Cruzalegui, Marco A. "Perceptions of Latin American Business Graduates as Related to Adequacy of Employment in the New York City Metropolitan Area during the Years 1965-1971." Ed.D. Dissertation, Columbia University New York, 1975. Determines whether immigrants trained in vocational or college business programs in the Caribbean and most of Latin America find employment in the New York City area related to their training. Subjects also identify perceived qualities or attributes that were both advantageous and disadvantageous to their ability to find suitable employment in the metropolitan area.

330.   "Jamaican Émigrés Bring Thrift Clubs to New York." *The New York Times* (19 June 1988): 34. Sect.1 Pt.2, Col.3. An immigrant's efforts to save money to buy a house by joining a savings club, or Susu, illustrates both the growth of these organizations and of New York City's Jamaican population in the 1980s.

331.   Jones, Alex S. "Black Papers: Business with a Mission." *The New York Times* (17 August 1987): 1. Sect.B, Col.3. Surveys various black-oriented newspapers, including the "New York Carib News," geared to the area's Caribbean community.

332.   Kalmijn, Matthijs. "The Socioeconomic Assimilation of Caribbean American Blacks." *Social Forces* 74 (1996): 911-930. Examines the earnings and occupations of Caribbean American men in the 1990 census and explores the generational differences (economically) among British Caribbeans and African Americans. Concludes that British Caribbean immigrant men achieve more, economically, than African American men and that these differences continue into latter generations. Also explores the comparative economic achievements of British Caribbean and African American men when compared to those from the French and Spanish-speaking Caribbean.

333.   Kasinitz, Philip. "From Ghetto Elite to Service Sector: A Comparison of the Role of Two Waves of West Indian Immigrants in New York City." *Ethnic Groups* 7 (1988): 173-203. Previous research indicates that while West Indian immigrants to New York City, prior to the 1930s, benefited from the growth of local black economic enclaves discrimination limited that success. Post 1965 immigrants, however, benefited significantly from the growth of the overall service economy, English language skills and a high percentage of female laborers.

334.   Kasinitz, Philip. "The Minority within: The New Black Immigrants." *New York Affairs* 10 (1987): 44-58. The large wave of West Indian immigrants to New York City, from 1965 to 1986, is explored in terms of immigrant impact on the labor force and local culture and its potential impact on city politics.

335.   Kleiman, Dena. "Educator Asserts Immigrants Do Not Threaten Job Market." *The New York Times* (8 May 1983): 24. Sect.1, Pt.1, Col.1. Speaking at a conference on "Caribbean Migration and the New York Labor Market," a South American scholar asserts that immigrants to the city help keep certain businesses alive rather than denying jobs to native workers. Another presenter asserted that contemporary Jamaican immigrants were from a higher social/educational background than those who arrived in the city before 1940. A third paper compared the experiences of Jamaican immigrants in London and New York.

336.   Light, Ivan H. "Rotating Credit Associations." Chap. 2 in *Ethnic Enterprise in America: Business and Welfare Among Chinese, Japanese, and Blacks*, edited by Ivan H. Light, 19-44. Berkeley, California: University of California Press, 1972. Rotating credit association use is seen as a major factor in the relative entrepreneurial success of West Indian and Asian Americans when compared with African Americans who lost this economic tradition. Accounts of these organizations in China, Japan, Africa and the West Indies provide background on West Indian use of these associations in the Harlem of the 1920s and 1930s, where West Indians had significant small business and real estate holdings.

337.   Marshall, Adriana. "New Immigrants in New York's Economy." Chap. 3 in *New Immigrants in New York*, edited by Nancy Foner, 79-101. New York: Columbia University Press, 1987. Characterizes New York City's immigrant

labor force during the 1970s, concentrating on West Indians, Latin Americans and Asians. Primarily manual laborers, they gained an increased role in a declining manufacturing sector. Statistical tables aid in comparing the labor force participation of these groups based on their origin and gender. Immigrant inflow into low-end manufacturing jobs fostered industrial competitiveness as well as deteriorated working conditions.

338.   Model, Suzanne, and David Ladipo. "Context and Opportunity: Minorities in London and New York." *Social Forces* (1996): 485-510. Studies and confirms the prediction that the United States, as opposed to the United Kingdom, provides more favorable opportunities for economic achievement of West Indian and other non-white immigrants, and particularly for men. Distinctions are made between the opportunities for foreign-born vs. native-born West Indians in both countries.

339.   Model, Suzanne. "West Indian Prosperity: Fact or Fiction?" *Social Problems* 42, no. 4 (Nov.) (1995): 535-553. Investigates the hypothesis that West Indian black Americans are more economically successful than African Americans are. Both labor force and earnings data for residents of the New York City area in 1970, 1980, and 1990, are explored as dimensions of the hypothesis.

340.   Palmer, Ransford W. "Caribbean Development and the Migration Imperative." Chap. 1 in *In Search of a Better Life: Perspectives on Migration from the Caribbean*, edited by Ransford W. Palmer, 3-16. New York: Praeger, 1990. Argues that the character of Caribbean development encourages circular migration of household units and remittances between the United States and sending countries. Although many Caribbean migrants were employed in their island nations, they sought out the United States in order to maximize household income. Few actually returned home to live in the Caribbean, as illustrated by settlement patterns of Jamaicans and other West Indians in New York State and City in 1980.

341.   Palmer, Ransford W. "A Decade of West Indian Migration to the United States, 1962-1972: An Economic Analysis." *Social and Economic Studies* 23, no. 4 (1974): 571-587. Surveys West Indian migration to the United States between 1962 and 1972, emphasizing primary economic variables that affected and were affected by the emigration of professional and technical workers. Statistical analysis projected that higher United States wages would continue to drain skilled labor from Jamaica. Data are provided in nine statistical tables (covering 1962-1971) that include number of professional and technical immigrants, occupational distribution of immigrants, and remittances from the United States to Jamaica.

342.   Palmer, Ransford W. *Pilgrims from the Sun: West Indian Migration to America*. New York: Twayne Publishers, 1995. An economic analysis of the migration of English-speaking West Indians to the United States, concentrating on the period since the mid-1960s. Settlement patterns (especially in New York City), employment and economic status issues (focusing on Brooklyn, New

York), and seasonal migration of farm labor to southern Florida are among the topics explored.

343.   Papademetriou, Demetrios G., and Nicholas Di Marzio. *Undocumented Aliens in the New York Metropolitan Area: An Exploration Into Their Social and Labor Market Incorporation.* Staten Island, New York: Center for Migration Studies of New York, Inc., 1986. A socioeconomic profile of undocumented Caribbean and other Western Hemisphere immigrants in the New York City region and Newark, New Jersey based primarily on early 1980s data. Considers issues such as gender and age, economic class, employment rates, and desire to return to home societies. Includes useful statistical tables covering documented and undocumented Caribbean immigrants to the United States from 1965 through 1983.

344.   Portes, Alejandro, and Alex Stepick. "Three Years Later: The Adaptation Process of 1980 (Mariel) Cuban and Haitian Refugees in South Florida." *Population Research and Policy Review* 5 (1986): 83-94. Compares the labor market absorption among these two 1980 immigrant groups with their respective immigrant nationals of the 1970s. Includes comparative statistics on socioeconomic characteristics such as age, marital status, and education; data on employment, income and poverty; and data on social networks, perceptions of discrimination, and participation in ethnic enclaves. Mariel Cubans found greater employment in the Cuban enclave in firms owned by Cubans and Anglo-Americans than did Haitians.

345.   Portes, Alejandro, and Alex Stepick. "Unwelcome Immigrants: The Labor Market Experiences of 1980 (Mariel) Cuban and Haitian Refugees in South Florida." *American Sociological Review* 50 (1985): 493-514. Uses statistical techniques to analyze the differences in labor market penetration of 1980 Mariel Cubans and Haitians who arrived in Florida and were admitted on a temporary basis. Valuable socioeconomic statistics cover issues such as educational achievement, English language ability, employment/unemployment, and income. Compared to the Cubans, Haitians reported almost no self-employment after three years. Gender appeared to be the main determinant of rates of unemployment.

346.   Portes, Alejandro, and Min Zhou. "The New Second Generation: Segmented Assimilation and Its Variants." *Annals of the American Academy of Political and Social Science* 530 (1993): 74-97. Studies the children of several post-1960 immigrant groups, including Haitians and English-speaking West Indians, in South Florida. Observes three basic forms of adaptation and factors that create vulnerability to downward assimilation. A survey of second-generation eighth- and ninth-grade students living in South Florida explored socioeconomic characteristics, self-identification, and career/educational aspirations in a climate of racial discrimination.

347.   Potocky, Miriam. "Refugee children: How Are They Faring Economically as Adults?" *Social Work in Education* 41, no. 4 (July) (1996):

364-374. A study of "the economic well-being of refugees who arrived in the United States as children" but who are now adults. Using 1990 Census data, Haitians and four other groups were examined. Compared to the others, Haitians and Nicaraguans faired poorly. The reasons for these outcomes are discussed as well as implications for policy and program development.

348.   Rohlehr, Lloyd. "Jamaicans in South Florida, Take a Bow!" *Caribbean Today* 7, no. 11 (1996): 27. Reports on an article in the Miami Herald, which highlights the economic achievements of Jamaican expatriates. Summarizes the role played by funds remitted to Jamaica, entrepreneurial skills of Jamaicans in South Florida, their household income, and home ownership.

349.   Salins, Peter D. "In Living Colors." *The New Republic* 204 (21 January 1991): 14-15. Recent immigrants of color, including Haitians, have filled needed jobs in low wage manufacturing and service industries in New York City. States that the city's ethnic profile means that politics do not revolve around race.

350.   Sol, Ahiarah. "Black Americans' Business Ownership Factors: A Theoretical Perspective." *The Review of Black Political Economy* 22 (1993): 15. Notes that in New York descendants of West Indian immigrants are more entrepreneurial than are their native black peers of equivalent educational backgrounds. Theorizes that this is partly due to the historical population dominance of the black slaves in the West Indies. West Indian captive laborers and their descendants did not compete with a significant white working class and therefore developed entrepreneurial skills. The opposite was true for blacks in the United States.

351.   Sontag, Deborah. "Haitian Migrants Settle in, Looking Back." *The New York Times* (3 June 1994): 1. Sect.A, Col.2. Profiles Haitian-American diversity that includes taxi drivers in New York City and successful medical doctors on Long Island. Includes a discussion of the minority status Haitians face as black foreigners and non-English speakers. The Haitian American community along Brooklyn's Nostrand Avenue forms a vital part of Brooklyn's ethnic fabric.

352.   Sontag, Deborah. "New Cabbies Reflect Change in the Mosaic of New York." *The New York Times* (23 April 1992): 1. Sect.B, Col.2. Taxicab drivers from the Caribbean were a significant part of the industry in 1992. However, as of 1992, immigrants from the Indian subcontinent had replaced West Indians as the largest number of applicants for taxi driver jobs through government agency channels.

353.   Sowell, Thomas. "West Indian Immigrants." in *Essays and Data on American Ethnic Groups*, edited by Thomas Sowell, 41-51. Washington, D.C.: The Urban Institute, 1978. Briefly surveys the socioeconomic status of West Indians in New York City and draws tentative conclusions for their relative socioeconomic success, as compared to native black Americans. Various statistical tables, based on 1970 census and other data, explore issues of West Indian education, income, and fertility.

Economic Life 33

354.	Stepick, Alex, and Alejandro Portes. "Flight into Despair: A Profile of Recent Haitian Refugees in South Florida." *International Migration Review* 20, no. 2 (1986): 329-350. Based on a survey, conducted in 1983-1984, of post-1980 Haitian refugees to South Florida. Individual background characteristics sampled such measures as age, marital status, and place of birth. Arrival and resettlement data indicate frequent detentions by immigration officials and limited family networks. Education and related data indicate modest achievements. Employment status and occupation statistics were grim. Data on beliefs included religion and perceived discrimination.

355.	Stepick, Alex. "The Haitian Informal Sector in Miami." *City & Society: Journal of the Society for Urban Anthropology* 5 (1991): 10-22. Argues that basically negative United States policy toward Haitians led to "widespread unemployment, low-paid, informal-sector wage-labor jobs, and unremunerative, small informal sector enterprises." Anti-Haitian prejudice is said to have limited "access to the formal wage-labor market" and prevented access to the broader community's market for Haitian entrepreneurs.

356.	Stepick, Alex. "Miami's Two Informal Sectors." Chap. 6 in *The Informal Economy: Studies in Advanced and Less Developed Countries*, edited by Alejandro Portes, et al., 111-131. Baltimore: Johns Hopkins University Press, 1989. Finds that Miami Florida's Cuban immigrant sector has become linked to the region's broader economy while the Haitian immigrant sector has become an isolated informal one. Between 1977 and 1981, Haitians experienced wholesale rejection in the Miami area. This is reflected in the underemployment and high unemployment levels of Haitians and their active exclusion from the garment and construction industries. Haitians constructed a gender-based separate economy fueled by survival strategies.

357.	Waldinger, Roger. "From Ellis Island to LAX: Immigrant Prospects in the American City." *International Migration Review* 30, no. 4 (1996): 1078-1087. The economic and political structures of the immigrant receiving areas of Los Angeles and New York City are said to shape immigrant outcomes. New York City's more diverse Caribbean immigrant population feeds into more advantageous ethnically based economic and political structures that affect immigrant opportunities in the labor market and politics.

358.	Waldinger, Roger. "The 'Other Side' of Embeddedness: A Case Study of the Interplay of Economy and Ethnicity." *Ethnic and Racial Studies* 18, no. 3 (1995): 555-581. This "case study of African American, Caribbean, Korean and white construction contractors in New York City" argues that "the embeddedness of economic behaviour in ongoing social relations...impedes access to outsiders." The study goes on to explore how African American, Caribbean and Korean contractors have developed different adaptive strategies to deal with these barriers erected by white ethnics.

359.	Waldinger, Roger. *Still the Promised City? African-Americans and New Immigrants in Postindustrial New York.* 1996: Harvard University Press,

1996. Based on an analysis of 1940-1990 census data and interviews with employers, workers, and union officials, the author explorers immigrant and African American economic behavior in New York City. The book focuses on six ethnic/nationality groups and traces the diverse economic patterns of native blacks and West Indians in terms of each group's place in "the ethnic queue, its niche creation, and its political clout." Two chapters trace the changes in native and immigrant shares of New York City jobs.

360.   Youssef, Nadia H. "The Contribution of Foreign-Born Workers to the Economy of New York." Chap. 6 in *The Demographics of Immigration: A Socio-Demographic Profile of the Foreign-Born Population in New York State*, edited by Nadia H. Youssef, 131-155. Staten Island, New York: The Center for Migration Studies of New York, 1992. Statistics for 1980 indicate the importance of immigrants to New York State's work force, with the Caribbean islands being the top supplier region. Worker skill level is analyzed generally by region of birth and by race/ethnicity/gender. Caribbean women ranked high both in upper skill occupations and service-related jobs such as household employment.

361.   Youssef, Nadia H. "Economic Characteristics of New York's Foreign-Born Residents." Chap. 5 in *The Demographics of Immigration: A Socio-Demographic profile of the Foreign-Born Population in New York State*, edited by Nadia H. Youssef, 95-130. New York: The Center for migration Studies of New York, Inc., 1992. Data compiled in 1980 are used to study inter-relationships of immigrant status, race and gender on the economic status of the state's foreign-born. Data indicate that non-Hispanic Caribbean and Asian immigrants had the greatest growth in new jobs in the 1970s. Caribbean and Asian women had the highest rates of employment among all immigrants and most Third World men had higher employment rates than men born in the United States. Region of birth and time of arrival in the United States offer additional views of economic activity.

FARM LABOR

362.   Craige, Tito. "Boat People Tough it Out: Haitian Immigrants Struggle to Survive in North Carolina." *Migration Today* 13, no. 2 (1985): 31-34. Chronicles the experiences of exploited Haitian migrant farm workers in North Carolina, during the early 1980s. Experiences of individual laborers illustrate the Haitians' litigious response to extremely low pay and poor working conditions as well as the efforts of governmental agencies and religious organizations to assist these migrant laborers.

363.   DeWind, Josh, Tom Seidi, and Janet Shenk. "The Cane Contract: West Indians in Florida." *NACLA Report on the Americas* 11, no. 8 (1977): 10-17. Examines the exploitation of Florida sugar cane contract workers, primarily those from Jamaica, St. Kitts and St. Lucia. The contract system primarily

benefited West Indian governments and Florida growers at the expense of contract laborers and to the detriment of potential American farm laborers and union activities. Through paycheck deductions and the threat of repatriation, Florida growers had maximum control of laborer productivity, discipline, wages, and grievance mechanisms. Includes data on West Indian agricultural workers, by state, for 1960 through 1976.

364.   Foner, Nancy and Richard Napoli. "Jamaican and Black-American Migrant Farm Workers: A Comparative Analysis." *Social Problems* 25, no. 5 (1978): 492-503. Comparisons of Jamaican migrant apple pickers, in New York State with native-black workers indicated that the former were both more productive and saved more money. Concludes that these differences were due to different perceptions of the value of the relatively low wages and different opportunities for upward mobility in home societies. Explorations of migrant camp organization, worker recruitment, and working conditions were found to be ancillary contributing factors affecting differences in worker productivity and thriftiness.

365.   Griffith, David. "International Labor Migration and Rural Development: Patterns of Expenditure among Jamaicans working seasonally in the United States." *Stanford Journal of International Law* 19 (1983): 357-370. Provides background on the British West Indies Temporary Alien Labor Program and tests the theory that earnings, etc. of returning migrant workers will aid the development of agriculture in sending societies. Research in 1982 tested the assumption that the program stimulated development in Jamaica but found no measurable long-term impact on Jamaican agriculture. With over half of migrant Jamaican farm workers' earnings remaining in the United States, the potential for rural development in Jamaica was limited to workers remaining in the program for four seasons.

366.   Griffith, David. "Peasants in Reserve: Temporary West Indian Labor in the U.S. Farm Labor Market." *International Migration Review* 20, no. 4 (1986): 875-898. Examines relevant legal issues, the United States farm market, and socioeconomic conditions of the Jamaican peasantry as primary migrant harvesters of apples in the Northeast United States and sugar cane in South Florida. The program's history demonstrates how American apple and sugar producers legitimated recruitment of migrant labor despite the availability of unemployed domestic labor. West Indian peasants constitute captive labor forces that consume most of their earnings, maintaining the living conditions that promote migration.

367.   Griffith, David. "The Promise of a Country: The Impact of Seasonal U.S. Migration on the Jamaican Peasantry." Ph.D. Dissertation, University of Florida (Gainesville), 1983. Compares sample Jamaican household populations of migrant and non-migrant laborers in the Northeast United States apple harvest and South Florida sugar cane industries. Few differences exist between the two groups; thus dispelling the theory that labor migrants returning from developed countries substantially aided the development of their home societies.

368.   Griffith, David C. "Social Organizational Obstacles to Capital Accumulation among Returning Migrants: The British West Indies Temporary Alien Labor Program." *Human Organization* 45, no. 1 (1986): 34-42. Finds that Jamaicans who migrate seasonally to the United States to work harvesting sugarcane and apples have difficulties accumulating financial resources.

369.   Hahamovitch, Cindy. "In The Valley of the Giant: The Politics of Migrant Farm Labor, 1865-1945." Ph.D. Dissertation, The University of North Carolina at Chapel Hill (Chapel Hill, N.C.), 1992. Explores the interventionist activities of federal agencies into farm labor relations in New Jersey, Georgia and Florida between 1865 and 1945. Most farm employer efforts to control the supply of available farm workers were directed toward blacks, including migrants from the Caribbean near the end of this period. Federal agencies aided this effort by replacing militant migrants with workers recruited from abroad under no-strike contracts.

370.   "'I Never Knew They Existed': The Invisible Haitian Migrant Worker." *Migration World Magazine* 15, no. 2 (1987): 17-21. Thousands of Haitian farm workers entered North Carolina annually between 1982 and 1987, as an isolated, poorly paid, and poorly treated workforce. Hard working, dedicated workers faced constant indebtedness to the company store and the working conditions imposed by crew bosses. Being lumped with black Americans added further stress to many Haitian migrant laborers.

371.   McGhee, Dorothy. "Apple Picker Blues." *The New Republic* (29 October 1977): 15-16. Reports on the conflict between apple growers, in New York and other states, with the United States Department of Labor, which sought to encourage the use of domestic workers in commercial apple orchards. The observer concludes that the growers preferred migrant Jamaican workers because they were a "captive," "submissive," "hard working" and "pliable" labor force. Using various tactics, the growers thwarted Labor Department efforts and obtained certification to import some 5000 Jamaican migrant workers.

372.   *Migrant Farmworkers in the Oak Orchard Health Service Area: A Descriptive Profile and Assessment of Health Care Needs and Economic Impact.* Buffalo, N.Y.: State University of New York, Buffalo. Regional Economic Assistance Center. ERIC, ED 294 707, 1984. A comparative study of individual farmworkers and family farmworkers from selected immigrant groups, which assesses demographic characteristics, health care status, and income spending patterns. Information included covers Jamaicans and native-born blacks.

373.   Tucker, Barbara M. "Agricultural Workers in World War II: The Reserve Army of Children, Black Americans, and Jamaicans." *Agricultural History* 68, no. 1(Winter) (1994): 54-73. Discusses the methods used to provide labor to New Jersey and Connecticut farms, during World War II. Among those methods were the use of Southern United States white and black migrant labors and federally controlled Jamaican labor.

374.   Watson, James, and Mattera Gloria. "Alcohol Use among Migrant Laborers in Western New York." *Journal of Studies on Alcohol* 46 (1985): 403-411. Surveys of African American and Haitian agricultural workers, in upstate New York, determined that camps composed mainly of family groups exercised more social control than those camps populated mainly by individuals living without families. This social control was reflected in different patterns of drinking behavior. Concluded that mechanized agriculture reinforced the use of homeless and troubled workers.

WOMEN IN THE ECONOMY

375.   Burgess, Judith Ann. "Women's Migration and Work: The Integration of Caribbean Women into the New York City Nurse Workforce." Ph.D. Dissertation, Columbia University (New York City), 1989. Research based on the view of migration as a system of cross-border labor supply. English-speaking Caribbean women are the unit of analysis and are seen as an international reserve of nurses imbued with the cultural norms of industrial societies. A complex set of organizational and cultural factors is explored as determining the status of these nurses in the New York City labor force.

376.   Colen, Shellee. "Housekeeping for the Green Card: West Indian Household Workers, the State, and Stratified Reproduction in New York." in *At Work in Homes: Household Workers in World Perspective*, edited by Roger Sanjek and Colen Shellee, 89-118. Washington, D.C.: American Anthropological Assoc., 1990. Federal immigration laws, requiring sponsorship by United States citizens, are found to direct many undocumented West Indian women into household/child-care work in the New York City area in order to obtain an employer's sponsorship for a "Green Card," which verifies the immigrant's legal residency. With household employer sponsorship for a United States government Green Card as the goal, these workers often face indenture-like conditions, performing low-status, low-paying tasks without the expected mutual respect. Having obtained legal status, interviewees express a feeling of freedom. Most employees leave their sponsor's employment and reinforce their connections with their immigrant ethnic communities.

377.   Colen, Shellee. "Just a Little Respect: West Indian Domestic Workers in New York City." in *Muchachas No More: Household Workers in Latin America and the Caribbean*, edited by Elsa M. Chaney and Mary G. Castro, 171-194. Philadelphia, Pa.: Temple University Press, 1989. American immigration policy is seen as the major reason West Indian women pursue sponsored domestic service so as to gain legal resident status. West Indian women, many having left children in the Caribbean, provided a new source of household workers after 1965. Many find this work, especially under "live-in" conditions, objectionable because it is reinforced by inequalities of class, gender, race, ethnicity, and migration. Employees find the lack of respect they receive from employers insulting. Employees cope by reinforcing their own

identities through systems of respect operative in their island countries and local New York City communities.

378.   Foner, Nancy. *The Caregiving Dilemma: Work in an American Nursing Home*. Berkeley: University of California Press, 1994. An ethnographic study of a New York City nursing home which focuses on the work of the nursing aides who were primarily women of color. Highlights the conflicts both among these aides and with other groups in the work place. Emphasized are the racial and ethnic differences dividing these groups who include Jamaican, Puerto Rican, and African American workers. However, many cases illustrated cooperation and friendship between West Indian and African American workers.

379.   Foner, Nancy. "Sex Roles and Sensibilities: Jamaican Women in New York and London." in *International Migration: The Female Experience*, edited by Rita J. Simon and Caroline B. Brettell, 133-151. Totowa, N.J.: Rowman & Allanheld, 1986. Analyzes the socioeconomic impact of the migration experience on Jamaican women in New York City and London, England. Differences between the sexes exist in patterns of immigration, occupational status, earnings and household roles in both cities. Despite many inequalities, Jamaican female immigrants find their experience beneficial in terms of independence; money earned, and shared household responsibilities with spouses. Racial and class discrimination enhances feelings of unity with Jamaican men as opposed to heightening feminist consciousness.

380.   Gordon, Monica H. "Dependents or Independent Workers? The Status of Caribbean Immigrant Women in the United States." Chap. 6 in *In Search of a Better Life: Perspectives on Migration from the Caribbean*, edited by Ransford W. Palmer, 115-136. New York: Praeger, 1990. Examines the economic role of Caribbean immigrant women in the United States, during the 1960s and 70s when many were "principal aliens" (i.e., those able to extend immigration privileges to others). United States Census (1980) data summarizes marital status, income, education, and occupational distribution by gender of immigrants from four Caribbean islands. Employment opportunities in the health industry and private households caused women to dominate this immigrant flow, but immigrant status, gender, and race limited their occupational choices and income.

381.   Johnson, Audrey. "Ethnic, Racial Attitudes among Professional and Managerial Black Women: Research Note." In *Female Immigrants to the United States: Caribbean, Latin American, and African Experiences*, edited by Delores M. Mortimer and Roy S. Bryce-Laporte, 143-156. Washington, D.C.: Smithsonian Institution, 1981. Data gathered from sampling black professional or managerial women in the New York City area tested hypotheses involving major regional differences among native blacks and the cultural uniqueness of West Indians. Data indicated distinct perceptual differences between Southern and Northern-born blacks, different perceptions of higher educational opportunity between native blacks and West Indians, differing perceptions of

family life styles between native blacks and West Indians, and different ethnic perceptions of class and racial discrimination.

382.   Lord, Mavis Rosetta. "Cross-Cultural Differences in Efficacy Expectations of Achievement Motivation between Women." Ph.D. Dissertation, Miami Institute of Psychology of the Caribbean Center for Advanced Studies (Miami, Fla.), 1993. Used standardized tests to establish differences in the need to achieve in three groups of women: African Americans, West Indians, and Caucasian. West Indian women scored closer to white American women on a "Need for Achievement Scale." Concluded that culture, more than ethnicity affected these women's need to achieve.

383.   Marshall, Paule. "Black Immigrant Women in *Brown Girl, Brownstones*." In *Caribbean Life in New York City: Sociocultural Dimensions*, edited by Constance R. Sutton and Elsa M. Chaney, 81-85. New York: Center for Migration Studies of New York, 1992. Discusses the immigration of female Barbadians, in the 1920s to New York City and their triple invisibility as black foreign women. Domestic work was the only avenue for their pursuit of middle class status, home ownership, and higher education for their children. Involvement in the Garvey movement demonstrated these immigrants' social distance from native black women.

384.   Model, Suzanne. "Caribbean Immigrants: A Black Success Story?" *International Migration Review* 25, no. Summer (1991): 248-276. When controlled for gender, an examination of 1980 earnings did not justify the opinion that West Indian Americans had higher earnings than African Americans did. While "Caribbean-born men experienced vast earnings disparities relative to white men," West Indian females earned the equivalent of white women.

385.   Nicholson, Marteen. "Migration of Caribbean Women in the Health Care Field: A Case Study of Jamaican Nurses." Ph.D. Dissertation, City University of New York, 1985. A study of Jamaican migrant nurses as independent factors in the migration stream who are affected by the "push-pull" of the immigration process. The structural nature of their lives as immigrants and their adaptation to their experience are other elements explored.

386.   Petras, Elizabeth McLean. "Jamaican Women in the U.S. Health Industry: Caring, Cooking and Cleaning." *International Journal of Urban and Regional Research* (Great Britain) 13 (June) (1989): 304-322. From the 1960s through the 1980s, Jamaican female immigrants filled a large percentage of the support level, health care positions in New York and other Mid-Atlantic States. Their work habits and training were major factors in their employment levels.

387.   Stafford, Susan H. "Haitian Immigrant Women: A Cultural Perspective." *Anthropologica* (Canada) 26 (1984): 174-189. Female Haitian immigrants to New York City, from the 1950s through 1977, are studied in

terms of the immigration process, integration into the work force and changes in Haitian domestic and cultural life.

Chapter 4

Education

401. Baldwin, Anne. "Foreign Student Profile. Research Report No. 86-16." 1986. ERIC, ED 269 111. Profiles foreign student enrollments in United States institutions of higher education, with a detailed examination of Miami-Dade (Florida) Community College (MDCC). National foreign student enrollments are noted by state, field of study and country of origin. Students from the Caribbean were among the three largest groups of foreign students enrolled at MDCC.

402. Ballenger, Cynthia. "Social Identities, Moral Narratives, Scientific Argumentation: Science Talk in a Bilingual Classroom." *Language and Education* 11, no 1 (1997): 1-14. Explores a Haitian bilingual education class setting involving a student-directed discussion format and student questions to encourage students' everyday language and idea exploration. Analyzes how students learn in this context.

403. Barnes, Grace M. "Patterns and Predictors of Alcohol Use Among 7-12th Grade Students in New York State." *Journal of Studies on Alcohol* 47, no. 1 (1986): 53-62. Examines various characteristics of alcohol and other substance abuse among 7th-12th grade students in New York State. Among the conclusions are that white and Native American students have higher rates of alcohol consumption than do West Indian, black American, Latino, or Asian students.

404. Berotte Joseph, Carole M. "A Survey of Self-Reports of Language Use: Self-Reports of English, Haitian, and French Language Proficiencies and Self-Reports of Language Attitudes Among Haitians in New York." Ph.D. Dissertation, New York University (New York City), 1992. Explores the use of Haitian Creole, English and French languages among Haitians living in New York City. Survey results indicate that the Haitian language predominates within

the social, personal, and religious lives of first generation Haitian immigrants. However, English predominates in the more formal settings of school and the workplace. These factors indicate increasing loss of vernacular French among Haitian immigrants as they gain proficiency in English.

405.   Bien-Aime, Joseph C. "Strategies to Improve the Self-Esteem of Ninth and Tenth Grade Haitian Limited English Proficient Students Through a Self-Concept Program." 1995. ERIC, ED 384 245. Describes the pre-testing and post-testing of self-concept of the target population. Describes the subsequently implemented ESOL techniques in connection with self-concept-enhancing group activities.

406.   Callahan, Walter. "Implementing the Professional Standards for Teaching Mathematics: Teaching Middle School Students with Diverse Cultural Backgrounds." *Mathematics Teacher* 87, no 2 (1994): 122-126. Discusses selected characteristics of Hispanic and Haitian students that may affect their abilities to learn mathematics. Provides classroom strategies to assist such students and suggestions to improve teacher awareness of the students' cultures.

407.   Cummings, Alban [John], et al. "Children of the Caribbean: A Study of Diversity." *Journal of Black Studies* 13 (1983): 489-495. Explores the causes of educational adjustment problems experienced by West Indian students in New York City and other American cities and the role played by teachers who do not understand the students' backgrounds. Language deficiencies, past schooling environment, experiences at home, and socioeconomic status are some of the causal factors explored.

408.   Cummings, Alban John. "Personal-Social Adjustment and Educational Achievement of West Indian Children in Selected Parochial Schools in New York City." Ed.D. Dissertation, Fordham University (New York City), 1979. An effort to compare the adjustment patterns and educational achievement of foreign-born West Indian students with American-born West Indian students. The major goal was to determine a possible relationship between length of schooling and the foregoing variables.

409.   Devine, John F. "Blackboard Jungle Revisited: The Semiotics of Violence in an Urban High School." Ph.D. Dissertation, New York University (New York City), 1990. Investigates coping mechanisms of a group of inner-city 9th and 10th graders, primarily migrants from the Caribbean, in a New York City High School impacted by street culture. Hypothesizes that many of these students will socially reproduce the drug culture of the neighborhood and resist externally imposed cultural models.

410.   Edwards, Ione Dunkley. "An Exploratory Study of Teacher Accommodation to the Cultural and Linguistic Differences of Jamaican Children Using a Clinical Supervision/Group Discussion Strategy." Ed.D.

sertation, Columbia University (New York City), 1983. A series of group discussion workshops along with clinical supervision techniques were used to alter teacher-accommodating behavior with Jamaican students. The change in teacher behavior resulted in more classroom participation by Jamaican students.

411.   Folkes, Karl C. "Issues of Assessment and Identification of Anglo-Caribbean Students in a Migratory Educational Environment." Paper presented at a Symposium on Education of Students from the Caribbean, Queens, New York, 25 May 1993. ERIC, ED 367 170. Examines the identification and assessment of the educational needs of West Indian immigrant students in New York City public schools. Due to policy failures, this population was over-represented in various remedial education programs. Recommends a model for understanding how people learn a language to better assess these students' educational needs. Also recommends a home language identification survey and assessment test.

412.   Foster, Charles R. "Instruction of Haitian Bilingual Children in the United States." *Language Problems and Language Planning* 4, no. 2 (1980): 101-106. Examines bilingual instructional problems for Haitian students in New York City and Miami, Florida. Such instruction is complicated by the predominance of Haitian Creole as the students' dominant language despite their parents' claim that French is dominant. Argues for a direct transition from Creole into English instead of via the French language.

413.   Foster, Joyce P. "The Role of the Academy in the Construction of Ethnicity among Black Caribbean Immigrants in the Urban United States: An Ethnographic Account of Commonwealth State College." Ph.D. Dissertation, Brown University (Providence, R.I.), 1997. Compared the experiences, interactions, and boundaries of African Americans and African Caribbean immigrants who were employed by or attended a four-year public college. The study investigated the "politics of racial/ethnic domination/subordination and the resulting stratification within the academy."

414.   Fouche, Marie. "My First Journey: A Haitian Immigration Story. A Learner-Centered Model Guide for Teachers." 1995. ERIC: ED 416 262. A teacher's guide developed by a division of the New York City Board of Education, that offers a learner-centered model in which the learner sees himself or herself in the story. The guide is based on the story of a young Haitian female, newly arrived in New York City. Based on the story learners should connect many of the experiences to language arts, mathematics, and social studies.

415.   Fradd, Sandra H. "School University Partnerships to Promote Science with Students Learning English." *TESOL Journal* 7, no. 1 (1997): 35-40. Explores a collaborative teaching-learning process between university professors and fourth grade teachers which seeks to promote science instruction

by building the teachers' understandings of the Haitian and Hispanic students' languages and cultures.

416.   Garrot, Carl L. "Phonemics within the Transitional Bilingual Program: From Haitian Creole to English." 1996. ERIC, ED 392 248. Studied the intrinsic and contextual difficulties of English spelling, for Haitian Creole-speaking kindergarten students, and the effect of phonemic awareness on the achievement of beginning spellers.

417.   Giles, Hollyce C. "Counseling Haitian Students and Their Families: Issues and Interventions." *Journal of Counseling and Development* 68 (January/February) 1990: 317-320. Uses the case study of a nine year old Haitian boy to discuss the various aspects of Haitian immigrant and refugee culture that cause adjustment difficulties for Haitian students and families to American schools. Factors covered include communication problems, the process of chain migration, illegal immigration status, and American expectations of parental involvement. Offers recommendations for counselor interventions.

418.   Gordon, Monica H. "West Indian Immigrants and the United States Education Process." Paper presented at the Caribbean Teachers' Association/Howard University/Phelps-Stokes Fund Conference, 23-35 August 1979. ERIC, ED 197 005. Provides an overview history of West Indian immigration and discusses this group's 1970s socioeconomic and education status in the United States. A discussion of immigrant settlement patterns and acculturation is followed by the conclusion that education difficulties of West Indian students are due to the failure of the American educational system and the West Indian community.

419.   Greene, Judy. "Project Avanse. Final Evaluation Report, 1993-94. OER Report." 1995. ERIC: ED 383 781. Evaluates a federally funded project in which Haitian-speaking high school students received instruction in English as a second language, native language Arts, and the academic areas of science, mathematics, and social studies. The project included peer tutoring and parent participation.

420.   Hall, R. M. R., and Beatrice Hall. "A Contrastive Haitian Creole-English Checklist." *The English Record* 21, no. 4 (1971): 136-147. The authors assert that New York City students from the French-speaking Caribbean speak French Caribbean Creole as their primary language and not standard French. Argues that affected schoolteachers must be aware of Creole language structure and sets out a broad outline of Creole grammar.

421.   Hawkins, B. Denise. "Haitian Educators Work for Education Reform in Time of Crisis." *Black Issues in Higher Education* 11 (6 October 1994): 24-26. Reports on a conference of educators that explored issues of Haitian education.

Includes discussions of problems faced by Haitian students and parents in New York City, Massachusetts and Florida. Issues addressed for these regions were bilingual students, teacher training and special education misplacements. Includes 1992-93 data on the distribution of limited English-proficient Haitian students, by New York City borough.

422.   Jarecke, Walter H. "Identifying the Vocational Potential of a Disadvantaged Population." *Vocational Evaluation and Work Adjustment Bulletin* 6, no. 2 (1973): 29-32. Argues that the socioeconomic characteristics of specific disadvantaged groups must be considered, when assessing the groups' vocational potential. Norms specific to Jamaican Americans and other minority groups were developed for use with standardized tests used to identify and evaluate vocational potential.

423.   "Learning About Haitians in New York State." Albany, New York: New York State Education Dept., Bureau of Bilingual Education, 1985. ERIC, ED 277 797. Geared to Haitian students and their teachers in New York State, this resource guide provides background on Haitian society, language, and culture. Includes a list of places of interest and sources of information on Haitians in New York.

424.   Leveque, Patricia Gill. "The Performance of English-speaking Caribbean-American Students in the Psychoeducational Process." Ph.D. Dissertation, Fordham University (New York City), 1992. Explores the educational assessment process of the indicated student population from referral to placement in special education programs in New York City. Specifically examines determinant achievement factors on cognitive and academic achievement measures; patterns of performance on an intelligence test; and the connection between reason for referral and program placement.

425.   Lewis, Leonard C. "Caribbean Immigrants in Higher Education: A Study of the Relationship among Their Learning Styles and Strategies, Achievement Motivation, and Academic Performance." Ph.D. Dissertation, Ohio University (Athens, Ohio), 1991. "Examines the relationship among learning styles and strategies, achievement motivation, and academic performance of Caribbean immigrant students" in selected two and four-year colleges. Based upon the findings, the study offered recommendations for the training in and utilization of effective learning strategies.

426.   Lombardo, Shari. "Career Awareness through Research in Science and Math Achievement of Haitian High School Students in New York City (Project CARISMA): Final Evaluation Report." 1994. ERIC: ED 382 465. Another study involving English as a second language for Haitian students. Multicultural education and parental involvement were emphasized. Some project objectives were met but the project failed to meet its goals for English as a second language and mathematics.

427.   London, Clement B. G. "Crucibles of Caribbean Conditions: Factors of Understanding for Teaching and Learning with Caribbean Students in American Educational Settings." *Journal of Caribbean Studies* 2 (1981): 182-188. Calls for American educators to know some Caribbean history and have sensitivity for Caribbean values and cultural patterns, when attempting to interact with students of Caribbean background. An understanding of Caribbean speech patterns, other communications issues, and learning styles versus learning abilities are other factors considered.

428.   London, Clement B. G. "Teaching and Learning with Caribbean Students." Paper presented at the Association of Caribbean Studies Annual Conference entitled "New Directions in Caribbean Studies: Facing the 80's." 2nd, Nassau, Bahamas, 17-18 July 1980. ERIC, ED 196 977. Discusses the need for the American educational system to consider the unique cultural needs and values of Caribbean students. In the context of a discussion of these students' background in the Caribbean and their values, the author offers suggestions to educators.

429.   Lynch, Robert E. "The Migrant Heritage Studies Kit: A Teaching Tool." *New York Folklore* 13, no. 1-2 (1987): 29-48. Describes a curriculum materials kit produced by a Geneseo, New York migrant center. The kit supplies teaching materials on the cultural heritage of Haitian, African American, and other migrant farm workers that was used with such workers in the 1970s and 1980s.

430.   Mace-Matluck, Betty J., et al. "Through the Golden Door: Educational Approaches for Immigrant Adolescents with Limited Schooling." In *Topics in Immigrant Education 3. Language in Education: Theory and Practice 91.* 1998. ERIC: ED 421 019. Provides information and guidelines to develop effective school programs for Haitian and other immigrant students with limited prior schooling. Includes in-depth information about the lives, backgrounds, aspirations, educational experiences, and needs of five Haitian American adolescents.

431.   Mattingly, Vera Wilcher. "Self-Esteem, Academic Adjustment, and Acculturation among Haitian Students at Kingsborough Community College CUNY." Ed.D. Dissertation, Fordham University (New York City), 1990. Investigates the relationship between acculturation, academic adjustment and self-esteem of Haitian students, at a New York City community college. Concludes that acculturation is significantly related to self-esteem and academic achievement. In turn, self-esteem was observed to be related to academic and social motivation as well as ease of transition to college.

432.   McKenzie, Victor M. "Ethnocultural Factors in Counseling with Male West Indian American Adolescents." Ph.D. Dissertation, Syracuse University (Syracuse, N.Y.), 1984. Researched the ethnic and cultural factors involved in

the intercultural counseling of English-speaking West Indian middle school students. Findings emphasized the need for counselor knowledge of their West Indian clients' psychohistory and cultural background and reluctance to seek outside help with personal problems. Developed an "Acculturation Predictability Grid" related to counseling outcomes.

433.   McKenzie, V. Michael. "Ethnographic Findings on West Indian-American Clients." Journal of Counseling and *Development* 65 (September) (1986): 40-44.   The sociocultural context counseling needs of West-Indian students are outlined, based on studies of nine male students. These students initially hesitated to enter counseling due to its cultural stigma within their peer group as well as the broader West Indian community and tended to view the counselors as stern parental figures.   Counselors must be aware of West Indian culture, especially traditional career goals, to be effective.

434.   McLaughlin, Megan Elaine. "West Indian Immigrants: Their Social Networks and Ethnic Identification." D.S.W. Dissertation, Columbia University (New York City), 1981. Education as a means of social mobility is determined to be the overwhelming belief of this immigrant group. Racial discrimination was a reported detriment to advancement. West Indian social networks of family and friends are seen as playing the overriding role in the pattern of migration and adaptation to American life.   Ethnic identification as being West Indian was observed to intensify in this multicultural setting and there was a minimal amount of self-identification with the overall black community.

435.   Michael, Suzanne. "Children of the New Wave Immigration: An Exploration." Chap. 11 In *Emerging Perspectives on the Black Diaspora*, edited by Aubrey W. Bonnett and G. Llewellyn Watson, 239-256. Lanham, Md.: University Press of America, 1990. The life stories of West Indian immigrant children in contemporary New York City are very different from those of their predecessors. Experiences separating from migrating mothers and problems of assimilation with reunited families in New York City, are related to post-1967 female dominated migration. Because most post-1970 immigrant children were pre and early adolescents, the school and the street became their main agents of socialization. A crisis of identity, measured in academic achievement and the transition to work, led to predictions that many students would be closed out of the primary labor market and join the underclass.

436.   Michel, Claudine. "Of Worlds Seen and Unseen: The Educational Character of Haitian Vodou." *Comparative Education Review* 40, no. 3 (1996): 280-294. Sees voodoo as an integral part of the daily life and cultural identity of Haitians and examines the voodoo belief system which emphasizes the importance of community and the collective self. Explored within this context are instructional means of transmitting religious/moral values, roles of teachers and learners, and evaluation of the learner's progress.

437.   Nero, Shondel J. "Englishes in Contact: Anglophone Caribbean College Students in Metropolitan New York." Ed.D. Dissertation, Columbia University Teachers College (New York), 1997. The 1970s and 1980s brought an increased need for New York City schools to educate immigrant students whose native language was Caribbean creolized English. This study of anglophone Caribbean college students examines their language, language and identity, language attitudes, and "educational responses to ethnolinguistic diversity."

438.   New York City Board of Education. "Ann Sevi Ak Tout Entelijans Elev Ayisyen Yo: Yon Seri leson matematik ak syans pou elev edikasyon jeneral ak elev edikasyon espesyal (4em-8em ane) = Tapping into Haitian Students' Multiple Intelligences: A Collection of Mathematics and Science Lessons for General and Special Education Students (Grades 4-8)." 1997. ERIC: ED 416 698. "In each lesson, the basic text, all exercises, and a glossary are in Haitian Creole and a linguistic summary in English is provided for the teacher, suggesting sample student interactions and teacher-guided responses for each of three levels (beginning, intermediate, advanced)."

439.   Olsen, Dale A. "An Introduction to Latin American and Caribbean Musics in Florida: Multicultural Approaches in the Music Classroom." Position paper. 1990. ERIC, ED 357 988. A cultural profile of Latin American and Caribbean musical traditions in Florida. Designed as an introduction for music teachers in that state, with the goal of incorporating these traditions into the classroom. Also encourages teachers in other regions to create similar profiles of comparable ethnic music.

440.   Polk County Public Schools. "Capitalizing on Culture through Competency-Based Adult Education." 1993. ERIC: ED 359 828. A resource book that describes the characteristics of Jamaican, Haitian and other minority adult school students in Polk County, Florida. "Includes strategies for reaching each of the minority groups, and suggests intended outcomes and learning activities for English, social studies, mathematics, science, and business."

441.   Portes, Alejandro, and Dag MacLeod. "Educational Progress of Children of Immigrants: The Roles of Class, Ethnicity, and Social Context." *Sociology of Education* 69, no. 4 (1996): 255-275. Reports on a study of second generation Haitian, and other, second-generation immigrant high school students. Finds that the socioeconomic status of parents, length of stay in the United States, and time spent on homework affected the students' academic performance.

442.   Pratt-Johnson, Yvonne. "Curriculum for Jamaican Creole-Speaking Students in New York City." *World Englishes* 12, no. 2 (1993): 257-264. Outlines some of the problems encountered in the New York City public schools by students who speak only Jamaican Creole and by those who teach them. The

study argues for a specialized curriculum and instruction for these students and makes suggestions for a model program.

443.   Prou, Marc E. "English Language Development of Haitian Immigrant Students: Determining the Status of Selected Ninth Graders Participating in Transitional Bilingual Education." Ed.D. Thesis, University of Massachusetts, (Amherst, Mass.) 1994. Studied the status of English language development among Haitian ninth grade students in Boston bilingual education programs. The results indicated that the students' effectiveness in reading and speaking English was almost equal after enrollment in the programs.

444.   Rorro, Gilda L., and Pamela J. Leggio. "A Handbook for Teachers of Haitian Students in New Jersey." Trenton, N.J.: New Jersey State Dept. of Education, Trenton. Office of Equal Educational Opportunity, 1984. ERIC, ED 266 227. A curriculum guide designed to provide teachers with information on the historical, social and cultural background of Haiti and Haitian immigrant students. Discusses immigrant adjustment issues and suggests ways of working with students and their parents. Includes stories, poems, and songs for classroom use plus one lesson plan for kindergarten students and one for students in grades 7 through 9.

445.   Rosenthal, Beth S. "The Influence of Social Support on School Completion among Haitians." *Social Work in Education* 17, no. 1 (1995): 30-39. Studies the social dynamics of completing school, based on interviews with Haitian high school students in a New York City suburb. Two case studies indicate that despite having characteristics of potential dropouts, most Haitian students complete school due to positive reinforcement from community and parents. Cases of dropping out were directly linked to the lack of parental support. School social workers are offered a school dropout prevention strategy based on the study's findings.

446.   Rounds, Connie C. "Instructing Our Newest Minority: The Haitian." *Action in Teacher Education* 5, no. 3 (1983): 49-53. Presents a sample curriculum guide geared to teaching Haitian students in Central Florida. The program was designed to emphasize the process of acculturation and the development of survival skills. Students participated in experimental activities, enhanced by skill reinforcement and review practice.

447.   Seligman, Linda. "Haitians: A Neglected Minority." *Personnel and Guidance Journal* 55, no. 7 (1977): 409-411. Presents a survey of adaptation issues and cultural characteristics of Haitians in an effort to enlighten teachers and student counselors. Immigrant legal status, language, race and inter-ethnic relations are among the adaptive issues addressed. Immigrants' rural origin, the role of extended families, marriage practices and career orientations are among the cultural characteristics addressed.

448.   Smith, J. Owens. "The Politics of Income and Education Differences between Blacks and West Indians." *Journal of Ethnic Studies* 13, no. 3 (1985): 17-30. Argues that racial prejudice and discrimination alone do not explain the education and income disparities between African Americans and West Indian Americans. Maintains that these differences are affected by the "politics of inequality" operational in each groups' homeland or place of migration. Finds that these politics of inequality differently affect each group's ability to acquire the needed human capital to compete successfully in a competitive economy.

449.   Sontag, Deborah. "Caribbean Pupils' English Seems Barrier, Not Bridge." *The New York Times* (28 November 1992): 1. Sect.A, Col.1. A linguist finds that speaking Standard English at home caused adjustment problems for many West Indian students. Although many succeed in regular programs, others flounder as misplaced members of special education classes.

450.   Verdet, Paule. "Trying Times: Haitian Youth in an Inner City High School." *Social Problems* 24, no. 2 (1976): 228-233. A study based upon teaching English and mathematics to Haitians at a New England inner-city high school. Findings indicate that learning to use English destroys much of the mathematical competence these students had obtained using French language and notational conventions.

451.   Webb, John Badgley. "Expectations of Haitian Parents in the Greater New York Metropolitan Area: Education and Occupations." Ed.D. Dissertation, New York University (New York City), 1986. Explores whether or not Haitian immigrant parents' length of residence in the United States or their amount of schooling affected the parents' opinions on issues involving bilingual education programs for their children.

452.   White-Davis, Gerald Elroy. "Adaptation of Jamaican Immigrants in American Schools: Problems and Possibilities." Ed.D. Dissertation, Columbia University Teachers College (New York City), 1992. Considers the complex nature of the adaptation process to New York City schools for Jamaican immigrant students and their parents. Dominant adaptation factors include the impact of the pattern of immigration on the parent and child and the required socioeconomic and educational adjustments. Suggests ways to facilitate these adjustments.

453.   Winer, Lise. "Intelligibility of Reggae Lyrics in North America: Dread Ina Babylon." *English World-Wide* 11, no. 1 (1990): 33-58. "An examination of the extent and nature of the intelligibility of Jamaican reggae song lyrics for native speakers of North American Standard English, black American English, Jamaican English Creole, and other West Indian Creoles." Two tests were administered to four groups of speakers, in an effort to determine the extent to which the message of the songs could be understood.

454.   Zephir, Flore. "Haitian Creole Language and Bilingual Education in the United States: Problem, Right, or Resource?" *Journal of Multilingual and Multicultural Development* 18, no. 3 (1997): 223-237. Focuses on how the home language of Haitian Creole-speaking students is used in the school system and the value attached to it in providing effective instruction. "Educators are urged not to misclassify Creole-speaking students as African Americans" and to incorporate Creole-speakers' linguistic and cultural perspectives in the educational process.

Chapter 5

Ethnicity and Race Relations

501.   Arnold, Faye W. "Ethnic Identification, Ethnicity, and Ethnic Solidarity in Los Angeles County's West Indian-American Community." Ph.D. Dissertation, University of California (Los Angeles), 1987. Studies the ethnic identification, ethnicity and ethnic solidarity among West Indians in Los Angeles County. Found that American-born West Indians had usually assimilated into the black American middle class, identifying themselves as black or Afro-American. Concludes that West Indian ethnicity is reconstructed when immigrants face race-related obstacles to economic mobility.

502.   Ashmeade, Roy W. "A Critical Investigation With a View to Address Tension Between African-Americans and Caribbeans at the Brooklyn Temple Seventh-Day Adventist Church." D.Min. Dissertation, Drew University (Madison, N.J.), 1990. A study based on efforts to establish a program wherein African Americans and Caribbean Americans can accept and respect their various cultural differences in a religious setting. The conclusion reached was that an understanding of the other group's cultural norms could lead to a decrease in antagonism toward different cultures.

503.   Bashi, Vilna, and Antonio McDaniel. "A Theory of Immigration and Racial Stratification." *Journal of Black Studies* 27 (1997): 668-682. Argues that racial stratification is very important in shaping the lives of all blacks in the United States, including immigrants from Africa and the Caribbean. Maintains, among other things, "that immigrants lose their ethnic identities as they are reconstructed into races..."

504.   Best, Tony. "West Indians and Afro-Americans: A Partnership." *The Crisis* 82, no. 10 (1975): 389-391. Considers the problems faced by black Caribbean American immigrants because of their immigrant status and their blackness. Argues that these immigrants should expand intra-ethnic cooperation

with native-American blacks and struggle for civil rights, economic stability, and political power.

505.   Biafora, Frank A. "Cultural Mistrust and Racial Awareness among Ethnically Diverse Black Adolescent Boys." *The Journal of Black Psychology* 19, no. 3 (August) (1993): 266-281. Reports on a survey of cultural mistrust and racial awareness among black adolescent boys in Miami, Florida. Major findings indicate that Haitians, especially the foreign-born, were more mistrustful of whites and had less racial awareness and pride in being black than did African Americans and other Caribbean Island students. Non-Haitian Caribbean Island students expressed the lowest levels of racial mistrust.

506.   Bryce-Laporte, Roy S. "Black Immigrants: The Experience of Invisibility and Inequality." *Journal of Black Studies,* September (1972): 29-56. Argues that the significant contributions of black foreigners to the United States were generally ignored because these immigrants suffered the double invisibility of being black and being foreign. West Indians did benefit from having lived in majority black communities where they had a history of land ownership and many became immigrant risk takers.

507.   Buchanan, Susan H. "Language and Identity: Haitians in New York City." *International Migration Review* 13, no. 2 (1979): 298-313. Also Published in: Sutton, Constance R. and Elsa M. Chaney, eds. *Caribbean Life in New York City: Sociocultural Dimensions.* New York: Center for Migration Studies of New York, 1987. 202-217. Studies the involved relationship of language (French vs. Haitian Creole) in the establishment of identity among Haitian immigrants. A dispute over which language should be used in a Catholic Mass illustrates the relationships between class, race, ethnicity, and politics in a particular Haitian community in Brooklyn, New York and the perceived importance of related ethnic/racial identities.

508.   "Campaign Launched to Raise Funds for Haitians." *New York Amsterdam News* (18 July 1992): 5. Col.1. A Haitian American civic organization launches a campaign to raise funds to improve the integration of New York City's 500,000 Haitians into American life.

509.   Cardo, Lorelynn-Mirage. "Development of an Instrument Measuring Valence of Ethnicity and Perception of Discrimination." *Journal of Multicultural Counseling and Development* 22 (January) (1994): 49-59. "Describes the Scale for the Effects of Ethnicity and Discrimination (SEED)." This instrument was designed to measure the capacity of ethnicity for self and of others as well as the perception of discrimination. The population measured was disadvantaged Hispanic, American black, and West Indian students.

510.   Charles, Carolle. "A Transnational Dialectic of Race, Class and Ethnicity: Patterns of Identities and Forms of Consciousness among Haitian Mi-

grants in New York City." Ph.D. Dissertation, State University of New York at Binghamton, 1990. The metaphor "I don't want to be black twice" is used to explore changing relationships between identity and social consciousness among Haitian immigrants to New York City. Factors such as race, class, and culture are explored as determinants of Haitian incorporation into American life.

511.   Charles, Carolle. "Transnationalism in the Construct of Haitian Migrants' Racial Categories of Identity in New York City." *Annals of the New York Academy of Sciences* 645 (1992): 125-144. Racial identities of Haitian New Yorkers are said to be strongly influenced by the Haitian Revolution, thus encouraging disaffiliation from black Americans. The drive to advance economically furthers this intraracial estrangement. Haitian migration is said to be based on transnational networks between North America and Haiti. Migration to New York was seen as a temporary condition, from 1957 to 1986. Haitians sought residence in New York for economic opportunity but found American racial conflicts alien to their self-identity as foreigners.

512.   Chierici, Rose-Marie Cassagnol. "Demele: Making It, Migration and Adaptation among Haitian Boat People in the United States." Ph.D. Dissertation, The University of Rochester (Rochester, New York), 1986. An examination of migration and adaptation processes of Haitian boat people who came to the Rochester, New York area between 1978 and 1982. In demonstrating how cultural norms motivate Haitian migration and restrict migrants' adaptation to American life, successful migration is identified as making it to society's mainstream. The concept of "demele" (to fight for survival) is the driving force behind the Haitian immigrant's lifestyle.

513.   Degazon, Cynthia Evonne. "The Relationship of Ethnicity, Social Support, and Coping Strategies among Three Subgroups of Black Elderly." Ph.D. Dissertation, New York University (New York), 1987. Explores methods of coping with old age among three black elderly subgroups in New Jersey and the New York City area. Results indicate that Haitians depend primarily on social support to cope with aging. Barbadians and black immigrants from the Southern United States are more likely to use various non-social coping mechanisms. Although each subgroup had a preferred method of coping with aging, there were no subgroup differences in social support.

514.   Foner, Nancy. "Introduction: New Immigrants and Changing Patterns in New York City." Chap. 1 in *New Immigrants in New York*, edited by Nancy Foner, 1-33. New York: Columbia University Press, 1987. Introduces a volume of essays that explore the reciprocal impact of post-1965 documented immigrants to New York City. West Indians were a major component of this immigrant flow and the city impacted their economic and employment status, sex roles, ethnic identity, and racial sensitivity. Immigrant backgrounds in turn impacted local neighborhoods, the city's cultural life, race relations, and the labor force.

515.   Foner, Nancy. "The Jamaicans: Race and Ethnicity among Migrants in New York City." Chap. 7 in *New Immigrants in New York*, edited by Nancy Foner, 195-217. New York: Columbia University Press, 1987. Studies conducted in 1982 demonstrated that ethnicity was the overall force shaping the identity of Jamaicans in New York City. The stigma of being black in America caused Jamaicans to stress their West Indian culture as being uniquely superior to that of native blacks. Feelings of superiority led to conflicts with native blacks and prevented strong racial coalitions. Despite some racial bonding, the tendency of whites to show preference for West Indians over native American blacks, enhanced a "divide and rule" syndrome.

516.   Foner, Nancy. "Race and Color: Jamaican Migrants in London and New York City." *International Migration Review* 19, no. 4 (1985): 708-727. Based on interviews of Jamaican immigrants to both New York City and London, England. Research determined that the prevailing racial climate was more advantageous for Jamaicans in New York City than in London. As part of a larger black minority in New York City, Jamaicans faced less discrimination than native American blacks as well as Jamaicans in London.

517.   Foner, Nancy. "Race and Ethnic Relations in Immigrant New York." *Migration World Magazine* 23, no. 3 (May-June) (1995): 14-19. As a result of immigration to New York City in the 1990s, black-white relations came to include a larger percentage of West Indians in the mix of blacks who were dealing with whites. The author maintains that significant ethnic relationships for most new immigrants are with other immigrant minorities. In this case, West Indians often have tense relationships with African Americans, but many friendships and alliances are also formed among these two groups.

518.   Foner, Nancy. "West Indian Identity in the Diaspora: Comparative Perspectives." *Latin American Perspectives* 25, no. 3 (May) (1998): 173-189. A comparative study of the formation of racial and ethnic identities of West Indian migrants to New York City and London, England. West Indian ethnic identity plays a more positive role in New York City than in London due to the social and cultural experiences of these immigrants. The development of these identities is also compared historically for New York City.

519.   Gladwell, Malcolm. "Black Like Them." *The New Yorker* 72 (29 April 1996): 74-81. Maintains that West Indian immigrants to America have had much more success defeating racism and achieving independent success than have African Americans, and implies that these black immigrants experience less racial discrimination than indigenous blacks.

520.   Glantz, Oscar. "Native Sons and Immigrants: Some Beliefs and Values of American-Born and West Indian Blacks at Brooklyn College." *Ethnicity* 5, no. 2 (1978): 189-202. A survey of students at Brooklyn College of the City University of New York bears out the hypothesis that immigrants from the En-

glish-speaking Caribbean share a belief in the value of hard work and have confidence in the political system. Faith in the work ethic was also found to be stronger among this group than among either native black or white students surveyed. The immigrant respondents also demonstrated a comparative lack of anti-white sentiment.

521.   Glick, Nina B. "The Formation of Haitian Ethnic Group." Ph.D. Dissertation, Columbia University (New York City), 1975. A review of Haitian history, culture and immigrant experiences in New York City form the background for this examination of attempts to link some Haitian New Yorkers into ethnic organizations in 1969-70. Ethnic identity results primarily from promotional efforts by political and other organizations like those examined herein. These efforts met with limited success because the American institutions involved allocated resources in a manner that discouraged ethnicity and negated strong leadership.

522.   Gonzalez, Nancie L. "Garifuna Settlement in New York: A New Frontier." In *Caribbean Life in New York City: Sociocultural Dimensions*, edited by Constance R. Sutton and Elsa M. Chaney, 150-159. New York: Center for Migration Studies of New York, 1987. (First published in: "*International Migration Review*," 133, no. 2 (1979): 255-263). Migration of Garifuna people (black Caribs from Belize, Guatemala, and Honduras) to New York City became significant in the late 1960s (30,000 by 1978). In an extension of past migratory behavior, these immigrants maintained their culture at home and abroad through reproductive and economic success and the remittance of money to the Caribbean.   Females joined a formerly male migrant tradition due to the availability of jobs. Ethnic identity and nuclear family ties were maintained in New York City while language and cultural background affected residential patterns.

523.   Gopaul-McNicol, Sharon-Ann Arlene. "A Cross-Cultural Study of the Effects of Modeling, Reinforcement and Color Meaning Word Association on Doll Color Preferences of Black Preschool Children and White Preschool Children in New York and Trinidad." Ph.D. Dissertation, Hofstra University (Hempstead, New York), 1986. In the spirit of the pioneering work of Kenneth Clarke and Mamie Clarke (1947), various intervention techniques were used in an effort to improve the positive attitude of black preschool children from Trinidad and New York City toward black dolls. Contrary to expectations, intervention techniques did not improve the rate of preference in either group.

524.   Gumbert, Edgar B., ed. "Different People: Studies in Ethnicity and Education." Atlanta, Georgia: College of Education, Georgia State University, 1983. ERIC, ED 230 475. Includes three papers dealing with multiethnic societies in the United States and Great Britain. The second paper considers cultural identity and assimilation of Caribbean Americans. Concludes that barri-

ers to assimilation have caused many Caribbean migrants to forgo assimilation and pursue "ethnic bargaining" for political strength and survival.

525.   Herlinger, Chris. "Culture Clash: Tensions between Koreans and Blacks in U.S. Cities." *Scholastic Update* (Teacher's Edition) 124 (20 March 1992): 16-17. Includes a discussion of causes of tensions between many Korean grocers in New York City and their black Caribbean customers.

526.   Hintzen, Percy. "Empowerment, Caribbean-Style: What African-Americans Can Learn from Black Immigrants." *The Utne Reader*, no. 56 (01 March 1993): 127-128. Argues that poor African Americans "would benefit from an alliance with black immigrants from Africa and the Caribbean." Emphasizes the community-based self-sufficiency of these immigrants and their concept of blackness as a positive attribute.

527.   Ho, Christine. *Salt-Water Trinnies: Afro-Trinidadian Immigrant Networks and Non-Assimilation in Los Angeles*. New York: AMS Press, 1991. Analyzes the assimilation of Trinidadians in Los Angeles, whose migration process depended primarily on networks of family and friends (fellow nationals). America's racial climate led Trinidadians to rely heavily on networking based on cultural and racial sameness. With few local organizations, the immigrants' primary social relations were transcontinental and multinational. These relationships and group insularity impede assimilation into America's mainstream but aid absorption into the indigenous black community. Concludes that only immigrant economic integration is desirable.

528.   Holder, Calvin. "West Indian Immigrants in New York City 1900-1952: In Conflict with the Promised Land." Chap. 3 in *Emerging Perspectives on the Black Diaspora*, edited by Aubrey W. Bonnett and G. Llewellyn Watson, 57-77. Lanham, Md.: University Press of America, 1990. Describes the antagonism of many West Indian residents of New York City, in the 1920s and 1930s, to the country's virulent racism and discrimination. This antagonism led most West Indian immigrants to refuse to seek naturalized citizenship in the 1920s and 30s, despite efforts of the black press and civic groups. Also described are the major conflicts between the larger society and West Indian followers of Marcus Garvey, other nationalist figures, the African Blood Brotherhood, Communists, and Socialists.

529.   Jean-Baptiste, Carline. "Haitian Ethnic Identity, Usage of Haitian Creole, Family Cultural Values, Level of Self-Esteem, and Locus-of-Control in Haitian College Students." Ph.D. Dissertation, Boston University (Boston, Mass.), 1991. Explores the relationship between Haitian-American college students' ethnic identity and the relevance of such elements as place of birth and the use of Haitian Creole to assimilate. An ethnic identity measurement scale was designed to quantify these issues and the relationship of ethnic identity to parental values.

530. Johnson, Violet Mary-Ann. "The Migration Experience: Social and Economic Adjustment of British West Indian Immigrants in Boston, 1915-1950." Ph.D. Dissertation, Boston College (Boston, Mass.), 1993. Explores how the pre-migration values and experience of early 20th century West Indian migrants to Boston, Massachusetts combined with the structure of Boston society to affect the outcome of the immigrants' community adjustment. Despite immigrant efforts to maintain their unique ethnicity, they became a part of the black indigenous community and were therefore limited occupationally, residentially, politically, and economically and subjected to racial discrimination.

531. Kasinitz, Philip. *Caribbean New York*. Ithaca, N.Y.: Cornell University Press, 1992. Argues that the significance of race and ethnicity, among West Indian New Yorkers, was primarily determined by outside forces. Pre-1930s West Indian immigrants identified themselves with native born blacks rather than as ethnic West Indians because race was the main determinant of opportunity. Ethnicity gained dominance in the 1980s because native blacks had replaced many West Indian political leaders and white politicians encouraged West Indian ethnic assertiveness. These differing racial/ethnic positions, Caribbean backgrounds, New York City community and organizational life, and immigrant economic roles are historically explored.

532. Kifner, John. "Tension in Brooklyn; Blacks March by Hasidim through a Corridor of Blue." *The New York Times* (25 August 1991): 36. Sect.1, Pt.1, Col.1. Focuses on a West Indian protest march against perceived police injustice and conflicts with Hasidic Jews.

533. Kim, Hugh K. "Blacks Against Korean Merchants: An Interpretation of Contributory Factors." *Migration World Magazine* 18, no. 5 (1990): 11-15. An analysis of ongoing boycotts of Korean American grocery stores in a Haitian/Jamaican section of Brooklyn, New York. Economic competition, ignorance of cultural differences, language barriers, and racial stereotypes are seen as feeding the boycott. Suggestions are offered to improve intergroup relations.

534. Lassiter, Sybil M. *Cultures of Color*. Westport, CT: Greenwood Press, 1998. A sourcebook of basic information about several cultural groups that constitute Americans of color. Each chapter covers topics such as the group's history, immigration, language, family structure, religious practices, and health issues. Includes separate chapters on Haitian Americans and West Indian Americans.

535. Leavitt, Roy L., and Mary E. Lutz. "Haitians in New York City." Chap. 3 in *Three New Immigrant Groups in New York City and the Human Services: Dominicans, Haitians, Cambodians*, edited by Roy L. Leavitt and Mary E. Lutz, 39-75. New York: Community Council of Greater New York, 1988. A cultural/

social overview of Haitian New Yorkers providing background information for interested community service groups. Migration history, statistics, residential patterns, and ethnic identity are traced through five phases (1957 to 1986). Issues of assimilation, class and color, language, family relations, sex roles, employment, and religion are highlights.

536.   London, Clement B. G. "On Afro-American and Afro-Caribbean Cooperation." *Journal of Ethnic Studies,* 8 no. 3 (1980): 142-147. Examines aspects of the Caribbean region that prompt migration of its citizens. Finds that views held by white Americans toward Caribbean immigrants inhibit more thorough assimilation of the latter group into American society. Calls for unification between African Americans and African Caribbeans, in response to shared circumstances of history, slavery, and ethnic identity.

537.   Lyons, Beverly Pauline. "The Differences in Social Service Utilization between Elderly United States Main Land (sic) Born Blacks and West Indian Born Blacks." D.S.W. Dissertation, Fordham University (New York City), 1994. Statistical analysis was used on 1990 sample data, collected in New York City, to determine if the ethnic groups involved utilized social service networks differently. Findings indicated no differences in service utilization but pointed out inherent cultural differences that could affect other aspects of help-seeking behavior.

538.   McAlister, Elizabeth A. "Vodou in New York City: New Creolizations: The Economizing of Ritual Time and Space in Haitian Religion." M.A. Thesis, Yale University (New Haven, Conn.), 1990. Examines the influence of the dominant American culture on the practice of "vodou" by Haitians in New York City. The segmentation of time, the lack of space, and Haitian American ethnicity have transformed "vodou" rituals while retaining basic principles of African Dahomean and "Kongo" spirituality. The author sees the spelling of the word as "voodoo" as pejorative.

539.   Millette, Robert E. "Social Stratification among First Generation Grenadians in Brooklyn: A Look at Adaptation to Deal with the New Society." Ph.D. Dissertation, New School for Social Research (New York City), 1982. First generation Grenadian immigrants are studied to determine whether New York provided the hoped for catalyst for social equalization or whether Grenadians retained their skin-color-based caste structure.

540.   Mirage, Lorelynn W. "Valence of Ethnicity, Perception of Discrimination, and self-esteem in High Risk Minority College Students." Ph.D. Dissertation, Fordham University (New York City), 1987. Explored the relationships between affirmative responses to ethnic group membership, perception of discrimination, and levels of self-esteem in multicultural high-risk college students. A perception of discrimination scale (measurement) revealed no significant differences between black American, West Indian, and Puerto Ri-

can students on self-esteem measures. Affirmation of ethnicity correlated positively with levels of self-esteem.

541.   Mittelberg, David, and Mary C. Waters. "The Process of Ethnogenesis Among Haitian and Israeli Immigrants in the United States." *Ethnic and Racial Studies* 15, no. 3 (1992): 412-435. Explores the formation of ethnic identity among kibbutz-born Israelis and middle-class Haitian immigrants to the United States. Both groups are ambivalent about the identities assigned to them by American society. Three social determinants are said to play major roles in the formation of ethnic identity, which is most inflexible for those groups defined by race. The American stigma of race, often leading to downward social mobility, leads Haitians to seek visibility as immigrants with dual racial and ethnic identity.

542.   Portes, Alejandro, and Zhou Min. "Should Immigrants Assimilate?" *Public Interest* (Summer) (1994): 18-33. Studied factors that eased or hindered the assimilation into America's mainstream of post-1965 immigrant groups, including Haitians and English-speaking West Indians in South Florida. Many second-generation Haitian students assimilated not to mainstream, but to inner-city culture. Thus the immigrants' environment often decided the course followed by their offspring. Second generation West-Indians were also considered to be at risk of assimilating to underclass culture. Access to the mainstream was often denied, despite levels of acculturation.

543.   Raphael, Lennox. "West Indians and Afro-Americans." *Freedomways* Third Quarter (Summer) (1964): 438-445. Explores the friction between West Indian immigrants to New York City and African Americans in the early 1960s. Maintains that much of this friction is due to mutual misunderstandings and lack of awareness of the real enemy. Implores the two groups to forego the prejudices imposed by mutual oppressors, learn from each other, and seek a common good.

544.   Regis, Humphrey A. "Communication and the Sense of Community among the Members of an Immigrant Group." *Journal of Cross-Cultural Psychology* 19, no. 3 (1988): 329-340. Statistical analyses of interviews seeking to determine which communication variables were significant predictors of a sense of community among Trinidadians and Jamaicans in Washington, D.C. The sources of information studied were friends and acquaintances of the immigrants and radio programs. The sense of community was predicted by different information sources for the two-immigrant groups.

545.   Regis, Humphrey A. and Leroy L. Lashley. "The Editorial Dimensions of the Connection of Caribbean Immigrants to Their Referents." *Journal of Black Studies* 22 (1992): 380-391. Tested the effect of news concentration, by a Washington, D.C. Caribbean community newspaper on Trinidadian and Jamaican immigrants' self-identification, either as members of the Caribbean immigrant community or as island nationals. Compared the number of news sto-

ries published about Caribbean immigrants in Washington, D.C. with news stories about Trinidad and Jamaica. Most of the news stories dealt with the overall Caribbean immigrant community. Readers of such media were likely to have a more regional and immigrant-community orientation than a specific home society orientation.

546.   Rieder, Jonathan. "Crown of Thorns: The Roots of the Black-Jewish Feud." *The New Republic* 205 (14 October 1991): 26+. Explores various racial and ethnic conflicts throughout New York City, especially the decades long conflict between Caribbean blacks and Lubavitcher Jews of Crown Heights, Brooklyn.

547.   Rieder, Jonathan. "Trouble in Store: Behind the Brooklyn Boycott." *The New Republic* 203 (2 July 1990): 16-17, 20-22. Looks at the circumstances surrounding the black boycott of two Korean produce stores in Brooklyn following a dispute between a Haitian female customer and a Korean merchant. Discusses the ethnic/racial, economic, and political forces affecting this boycott in a heavily Haitian part of Brooklyn, New York.

548.   Rumbaut, Ruben G. "The Crucible within: Ethnic Identity, Self-Esteem, and Segmented Assimilation among Children of Immigrants." *International Migration Review* 28, no. 4 (1994): 748-794. A 1992 study of the psychosocial adaptation of teenage immigrants from Asia, Latin America, and the Caribbean living in the San Diego, California and Miami, Florida regions. Various paths led to the ethnic identities described and statistically analyzed. Different patterns of ethnic self-identity existed among the three nationality groups but analysis showed that gender, country of birth, perceptions of discrimination, school location, and parental self-identification strongly affected ethnic self-identification of the students.

549.   Sansaricq, Rev Guy. "The Haitian Apostolate in Brooklyn." *Migration Today* 7, no. 1 (1979): 22-25. Describes the work of Roman Catholic priests, with Haitians in 1970s' Brooklyn, where some priests were attached directly to parishes and others lived in area apartments.   Those attached to parishes normally lived in the rectory near the church.   Those who lived in area apartments were often more available to assist with community, personal, and family matters as well as spiritual needs, including compiling a Creole hymnal, than the parish priests. Some parish priests created community service centers. The large percentage of undocumented migrants and the unique Haitian/African culture affected services provided.

550.   Schiller, Nina G. "All In the Same Boat? Unity and Diversity in Haitian Organizing in New York." In *Caribbean Life in New York City: Sociocultural Dimensions*, edited by Constance R. Sutton and Elsa M. Chaney, 182-201. New York: Center for Migration Studies of New York, 1987. Analyzes four phases of

organizational efforts by Haitian New Yorkers, that occurred between 1957 and 1984 that were both unifying and divisive. Class and political divisions dominated the first phase with race the major unifier. The second phase responded to American ethnic politics. The localization of political spoils and refugee issues dominated the third phase, while religious, occupational or Caribbean identity dominated the fourth phase. While itself plagued by class divisions, the Haitian American
community's efforts shifted between competition for power in the United States and efforts to change Haiti.

551.   Schiller, Nina G. et al. "Exile, Ethnic, Refugee: The Changing Organizational Identities of Haitian Immigrants." *Migration World Magazine* 15, no. 1 (1987): 7-11. Members of Haitian-American organizations were interviewed to determine organizational effect on group identification as either an ethnic minority or as political refugees. For various reasons 1957-60 migrants identified as political exiles, and 1960-72 migrants sought invisibility, while 1965-72 migrants sought ethnic identification. From 1971-81 these organizations publicly ignored Haitian politics while championing boat people whose refugee status was generally rejected. Thus organizational activities and identities probably affected refugee status of the boat people.

552.   Sims, Calvin. "Black Customers, Korean Grocers: Need and Mistrust; Shoppers Complain of Hostile Treatment, But Choices Are Few." *The New York Times* (17 May 1990): 1. Sect.B, Col.2. Discusses the conflict between many black customers, often of Caribbean descent, and Korean immigrant merchants in Brooklyn, New York neighborhoods.

553.   Smikle, Patrick. "Carib Immigrants, African-Americans Still Divided." *Caribbean Today* 9, no. 3 (1998): 13-14. Interviews with various Caribbean American immigrants point to issues of misunderstanding and tension with native African Americans. Interviews in South Florida and New York point out attitudes and opinions that feed this tension. One interviewee, however, points to political cooperation between the groups.

554.   Spurling, John Jasper. "Social Relationships between American Ne-groes and West Indian Negroes in a Long Island Community. An Exploratory Examination of Intra-Group Relationships in the Addisleigh Park Neighborhood of St. Albans, Long Island, New York." Ph.D. Dissertation, New York University (New York City), 1962. This study demonstrated that there was minimal cross-group contact between West Indian black and indigenous African American families in this Long Island community during the 1950s. Furthermore, length of residence did nothing to promote social interactions.

555.   Stafford, Susan B. "The Haitians: The Cultural Meaning of Race and Ethnicity." in *New Immigrants in New York*, edited by Nancy Foner, 131-158. New York: Columbia University Press, 1987. Examines the meanings and per-

ceptions of race and ethnicity among Haitians in New York City, and the social/behavioral consequences of these interpretations. These issues are placed in context by reviewing the history of Haitian immigration to New York City, their settlement patterns in neighborhoods of three city boroughs, and the role of voluntary associations and other social networks. Racial issues are seen as motivating New York Haitians to emphasize a culturally and linguistically French ethnicity. This emphasis on ethnic identity affects relationships with whites, native blacks, and other immigrants from the Caribbean.

556.   Stepick, Alex, and Alejandro Portes. *City on the Edge: The Transformation of Miami*. Berkeley: University of California Press, 1993. Explores tense inter-ethnic group relations in Miami, Florida in the context of the growth of its Cuban and Haitian communities in the 1970s and 80s. Haitians are seen as facing a triple subordination to Anglos, Latinos, and native American blacks. Cultural differences and comparable economic distress are seen as the prime causes of Haitian antagonisms toward the native black community.

557.   Sutton, Constance R. and Susan R. Makiesky. "Migration and West Indian Racial and Ethnic Consciousness." In *Migration and Development: Implications for Ethnic Identity and Political Conflict*, edited by Helen I. Safa and Brian M. Du Toit, 113-144. Chicago: Mouton, 1975. Also Published in: Sutton, Constance R. and Elsa M. Chaney, eds. *Caribbean Life in New York City: Sociocultural Dimensions*. New York: Center for Migration Studies of New York, 1987. 92-115. West Indian migration to Britain and New York City is explored as a bi-directional phenomenon that fosters a positive black identity both in migrant and sending communities. Concentrating on Barbadians, the study finds that migrants to Britain maintained their ethnic identity but gained a broader African-Asian third-world identity. Migrants to New York City were said to have been forced to reinterpret their identity as part of a larger black minority. Both migrant groups developed a heightened Caribbean consciousness that was re-transmitted to communities in Barbados.

558.   Taylor, Dorceta Ernesthene. "Determinants of Leisure Participation: Explaining the Different Rates of Participation in African-Americans, Jamaicans, Italians and Other Whites in New Haven." Ph.D. Dissertation, Yale University (New Haven, Conn.), 1991. This study determined that the independent variables of ethnic identity, sex, family, friends, marital status, and neighborhood residence significantly affected neighborhood park utilization. It also found that African-Americans and Jamaicans identified more with their ethnic groups in leisure pursuits than did Italians or other whites.

559.   Taylor, Dorothy L., and Frank A. Biafora Jr. "Racial Mistrust and Disposition to Deviance among African American, Haitian, and Other Caribbean Island Adolescent Boys." *Law and Human Behavior* 18, no. 3 (1994): 291-303. Based on a 1990 survey of middle school boys living in South Florida

that tested the correlation between racial mistrust and delinquent behavior. Questions assessed students' perceptions of the law and their willingness to commit crimes or abuse drugs. Statistical analysis indicated a strong correlation between mistrust of whites, especially teachers, and tendency to deviance.

560.   Thompson, Jonathan Alfred. "Cross-Cultural Ministry in a Pluralistic Religious Community." D. Min. Dissertation, Hartford Seminary (Hartford, Conn.), 1986. Studied the scope of diversity between West Indian and black American members of a particular church that was ethnically polarized. Developed theories and an active plan of reconciliation. A project-developed evaluation process measured effectiveness of the project. Differences between the two cultural groups and the progress of their movement to reconciliation were measured by a standardized test.

561.   "Three Brooklyn Museums to Explore Crown Hts. Roots, and Nerves." *The New York Times* (3 January 1993): 26. Sect.1, Col.1. Describes a three-museum project designed to trace the history and relationships of three ethnic/racial groups in Brooklyn, New York's Crown Heights neighborhood. The groups discussed were African Americans, Caribbean Americans, and Lubavitch Jews.

562.   Vickerman, Milton [Dave]. *Crosscurrents: West Indian Immigrants and Race*. New York: Oxford University Press, 1999. Presents personal racial experiences of West Indian immigrants living in New York City based on interviews of Jamaicans. Of particular emphasis here is the West Indian reaction to America's emphasis on race and these immigrants' efforts to both distance themselves from and identify with African Americans.

563.   Vickerman, Milton Dave. "The Responses of West Indian Men towards African-Americans: Distancing and Identification." Ph.D. Dissertation, New York University (New York City), 1992. Concludes that many West Indian men in New York City emphasize their ethnicity and distance themselves from African Americans on a personal level. However West Indians are said to identify strongly with African Americans on broader issues affected by race. The researcher concludes that West Indian men therefore attempt to combine distancing and identification in a "paternalistic ideology."

564.   Waldinger, Roger. "Beyond Nostalgia: The Old Neighborhood Revisited." *New York Affairs* 10 (1987): 1-12. Finds that post-1965 immigrants to New York City have leapfrogged the immigrant neighborhoods of their early 20th century predecessors. Although better quality housing is available, West Indians have still been primarily restricted to sharply segregated black neighborhoods. The growth of West Indian immigrants has heightened ethnic awareness and social distances from African Americans.

565.   Waters, Mary [C]. "Ethnic and Racial Identities of Second-Generation Black Immigrants in New York City." *International Migration Review* 28, no. 4 (1994): 795-820. Surveyed the racial and ethnic identities adopted by a group of adolescent second generation West Indians (including Haitians) living in New York City. Compared those identities with first generation immigrants from the same countries. Different perceptions of American race relations and economic opportunities affected these identities. Assimilation of second generation black immigrants was said to be affected by race and class and interaction with various peer groups.

566.   Waters, Mary C. "The Intersection of Gender, Race, and Ethnicity in Identity Development of Caribbean American Teens." In *Urban Girls: Resisting Stereotypes, Creating Identities*, edited by Bonnie J. Ross Leadbeater and Niobe Way, 65-81. New York: New York University Press, 1996. Examines the complexities of racial and ethnic identities for the adolescent children of Caribbean immigrants in New York City. Discusses how race relations in America shape and alter the minority immigrant experience. Also explores the types of identities adopted by inner-city teens and the factors that affect girls as opposed to boys.

567.   Woldemikael, Tekle M. [Teklemariam]. *Becoming Black American: Haitians and American Institutions in Evanston, Illinois*. New York: AMS Press, 1990. Surveys the adaptability of Haitian immigrants in Evanston, Illinois in light of the identity given to them by the majority and minority communities. Community life, migration patterns, and education are explored as parts of Haitian immigrant efforts to escape the lower class status ascribed to "most" native American blacks. Differences in first and second-generation immigrants indicate a melding into a black American identity that was reflected in America's economic caste system.

568.   Woldemikael, Teklemariam. "Maintenance and Change of Status in a Migrant Community: Haitians in Evanston, Illinois." Ph.D. Dissertation, Northwestern University (Evanston, Illinois), 1980. Examines how Haitians adapt to a socially and racially stratified American society and how American institutions adapt to Haitians categorized as blacks in an American context. Finds that Haitians create their own marginal community and identity structure, with second generation Haitians becoming more African American. The host society incorporates the migrants into an existing structure through social and political institutions.

569.   Woldemikael, Tekle M. [Teklemariam]. "Opportunity versus Con-straint: Haitian Immigrants and Racial Ascription." *Migration Today* 13, no. 4 (1985): 7-12. Studies the interaction of Haitian immigrants, native American blacks and whites in a Midwestern city (Evanston, Illinois), as does the author's longer 1980 dissertation. Emphasizes reasons for Haitian migration, whites' po-

sitions as societal mediators, Haitian status versus African American status, and social distancing.

570.   Youssef, Nadia H. "Nationality, Ethnicity and Race in the Demography of Immigration." Chap. 3 in *The Demographics of Immigration: A Socio-Demographic Profile of the Foreign-Born Population in New York State*, edited by Nadia H. Youseff, 51-74. Staten Island, New York: The Center for Migration Studies of New York, Inc., 1992. Studies the shifts in national origin, ethnic, and racial composition of New York State's post-1965 foreign-born population. Tables illustrate that Asian and Caribbean countries supplied most of the state's immigrants in the mid-1980s and that they arrived in larger numbers from more Caribbean countries than either California or the entire nation received. Jamaica, Guyana and Haiti supplied most of the city's foreign-born residents from 1975 to 1980. Three city boroughs (counties) stand out in a discussion of the residential distribution of the city's foreign-born.

571.   Zephir, Flore. *Haitian Immigrants in Black America: A Sociological and Sociolinguistic Portrait*. Westport, Conn.: Bergin & Garvey, 1996. An examination of the process of ethnic identity formation among Haitian New Yorkers that focuses on causal factors of identity formation. Finds that while United States society sees Haitians as part of a homogeneous black population, Haitians employ various criteria of ethnicity (primarily languages) to retain their "otherness." Haitian immigrants also retain more of a tie to Haitian than to American politics.

Chapter 6

Family Relationships

601.   Bonnett, Aubrey W. "The New Female West Indian Immigrant: Dilemmas of Coping in the Host Society." Chap. 7 in *In Search of a Better Life: Perspectives on Migration from the Caribbean*, edited by Ransford W. Palmer, 139-148. New York: Praeger, 1990. Analyzes the social and psychological traumas caused by the female-dominated West Indian immigration to the United States in the 1970s. Migrating alone, leaving children and spouses behind, often led to separation anxieties, neglect of personal needs, and difficult social relationships. Difficulties also surrounded children's caregivers back home. Children, reunited with mothers in the United States, often faced difficulties relating to their mothers and the American school systems. Finally, strains often developed between spouses once reunited in the United States.

602.   Brome, Henderson LeVere. "A Study of the Assimilation of Barbadian Immigrants in the United States with Special Reference to the Barbadians in New York." Ed.D. Dissertation, Columbia University Teachers College (New York City), 1978. An investigation into the intensity of adjustment to American life by Barbadian immigrants to New York City. The study concludes that these immigrants assimilated enough for basic survival but retained crucial Barbadian family relations and social institutions that form barriers to more complete assimilation into American society.

603.   Buchanan, Susan H. "Haitian Women in New York City." *Migration Today* 7 (1979): 19-39. Haitian women enjoy new freedom in their ability to find work in New York City and establish their independence. However, they are often forced to accept menial positions and have the added burden of domestic chores at home. Married couples report more successful relationships if they migrate together. However marital relations were strained when motherhood and various cultural restraints were emphasized for women who had attained some economic independence in New York.

604.   Burgess, Judith and James-Gray Meryl. "Migration and Sex Roles: A Comparison of Black and Indian Trinidadians in New York City." In *Female Immigrants to the United States: Caribbean, Latin American, and African Experiences*, edited by Delores M. Mortimer and Roy S. Bryce-Laporte, 85-111. RIIES Occasional Papers, No. 2. Washington, D.C.: Smithsonian Institution, 1981. Based on a 1977 study exploring choices and gender-related adjustment experiences of black and Indian Trinidadian migrants to New York City. This primarily female post-1960 migrant flow is explored as to the effect of different ethnic traditions on employment and educational aspirations; the role of marriage and the family; social relationships; and the roles of women at work and at home. The socioeconomic mobility of the migrant family, in terms or sex roles and racial minority status, is also examined.

605.   Desantis, L. and D. N. Ugarriza. "Potential for Intergenerational Conflict in Cuban and Haitian Immigrant Families." *Archives of Psychiatric Nursing* 9, no. 6 (1995): 354-364. This survey of Cuban and Haitian immigrant mothers explores how the families of these two cultural groups differ on sociodemographics, concepts of children, and various childrearing beliefs and practices.

606.   Fjellman, Stephen M., and Hugh Gladwin. "Haitian Family Patterns of Migration to South Florida." *Human Organization* 44, no. 4 (1985): 301-312. Maintains that the organization of the Haitian extended family enables Haitians in Florida to survive, and in some cases to prosper, under very difficult circumstances. Their concept of family includes various kinship and fictive kinship ties, extending to different communities and cities, and available for mutual support. Seven family histories that serve as case studies include examples of the multinational family and women's pivotal roles in migration networks.

607.   Foner, Nancy. "The Immigrant Family: Cultural Legacies and Cultural Change." *International Migration Review* 31, no. 4 (1997): 961-975. Explores how first generation immigrants to the United States transform their family relationships, based on old and new influences. Surveys these pre and post-migration influences on South Asian, Dominican, and Jamaican families and concludes that new family patterns emerge from their convergence.

608.   Fouron, Georges Eugene. "Patterns of Adaptation of Haitian Immigrants of the 1970s in New York City." Ed.D. Dissertation, Columbia University Teachers College (New York City), 1985. Structural elements of the sending and receiving societies are seen as causal factors in the assimilation of Haitian immigrants to America in the 1970s. Whereas younger immigrants identified with American society, older Haitians saw themselves as exiles rather than immigrants. Therefore this latter group failed to adapt to American society and that society's view of them as members of the overall black minority. These

age-based differences caused major tensions within Haitian migrant families and the further destabilization of the broader Haitian community.

609.   Gopaul-McNicol, Sharon-Ann [Arlene]. *Working With West Indian Families*. New York: The Guilford Press, 1993. Analyzes historical, cultural, educational, and psychological characteristics of West Indian and West Indian-American families for the benefit of psychologists and educators. Appendices include four non-standardized measurement scales used in the study: "West Indian Comprehensive Assessment Battery," "The Immigrant Self-Concept Scale," "Immigrant Attitude Survey," and the "West Indian Attitude Survey."

610.   Ho, Christine G. T. "The Internationalization of Kinship and the Feminization of Caribbean Migrants: The Case of Afro-Trinidadian Immigrants in Los Angeles." *Human Organization* 52, no. 1 (1993): 32-40. Studies the recycling and international network nature of female Trinidadian immigrants in Los Angeles. The elasticity of Caribbean families is reflected through immigrants' children being cared for in sending societies, international kin networks, women's primacy in these networks, and international travel (especially to Trinidad's Carnival) as social connectors. The intricate family ties maintained by one Trinidadian international family is illustrated through informal adoption, the primary binding agent with the homeland.

611.   Lacovia, R. M. "Migration and Transmutation in the Novels of McKay, Marshall and Clarke." *Journal of Black Studies* 7 (1977): 437-454. Examines the portrayal of Caribbean immigrants to North America in the works of three novelists. In these works "permissiveness, individualism...and [one's] circumstance characterize the community." These immigrants, in geographical motion, seek magical vertical social mobility in America. This mobility includes the importance of owning property. Immigration laws requiring marriage are seen as eliminating casual living arrangements. The male is often defined in relation to the preferred female immigrant and thus loses self-esteem.

612.   Larmer, Brook. "The Barrel Children." *Newsweek* 127 (19 February) (1996): 45-46. Reports on children left behind in Jamaica, when their mothers have immigrated to the United States to find employment. The children receive periodic cardboard barrels of clothing and money and often live with relatives. Many of the children are lonely and unsupervised, experience physical and sexual abuse, and drift into street gangs.

613.   Malcolm, Joan A. "Maternal Separation and Bonding, Perceived Social Support, Anxiety and Depression in Caribbean Immigrant College Students." Ph.D. Dissertation, Fordham University (New York City), 1995. Investigated the relationship between maternal bonding and separation in childhood and depression and anxiety in adulthood for a group of Caribbean immigrants living in New York City. This group was studied because Caribbean migration is female-dominated and leads to frequent mother-child separations.

614.   Maynard, Edward Samuel. "Endogamy among Barbadian Immigrants to New York City: An Exploratory Study of Marriage Patterns and Their Relationship to Adjustment to an Alien Culture." Ph.D. Dissertation, New York University (New York City), 1972. Investigates the general tendency of Barbadian immigrants to marry within their own ethnic/national group and to reject marriage with indigenous blacks. This rejection is due to immigrant belief that the black indigenous group holds a lower social position.

615.   McCallion, Philip, et al. "Exploring the Impact of Culture and Acculturation on Older Families Caregiving for Persons with Developmental Disabilities." *Family Relations* 46, no. 4 (1997): 347-357. Cultural issues in caring for persons with developmental disabilities are explored for various ethnic communities, including Haitian Americans. Some of the family caregiving themes included are what family members expect of each other, cultural values important to family members, and family willingness to accept services from outside the family.

616.   McPherson-Blake, Patricia C. "Psychosocial Factors Associated with the Immigration of Haitians and Jamaicans to South Florida and Changes in Their Parental Roles." Ph.D. Dissertation, Barry University School of Social Work (Miami Shores, Fla.), 1991. Studies the cultural transition, especially changing parental roles, of first and second-generation Haitian and Jamaican residents of South Florida. Concludes that although Haitians adapted better to the United States, they retained their more conservative child rearing practices. The availability of support systems aided the adjustment of both nationality groups.

617.   O'Sullivan, Sean Patrick. "A Sociocultural Analysis of Family and Friendship Influences on Teenage Deviance." D.S.W. Dissertation, Columbia University (New York City), 1981. The roles of parental discipline and sibling friendship networks are seen as major causes of teenage deviance in this comparative analysis of groups of West Indian, American black, and American white families in the Bedford Stuyvesant area of Brooklyn, New York. Concludes that West Indian youths were less deviant and less disposed to use drugs than the other two groups studied.

618.   Oswald, L. R. "Culture Swapping: Consumption and the Ethnogenesis of Middle-Class Haitian Immigrants." *Journal of Consumer Research* 25, no. 4 (March) (1999): 303-318. An ethnographic study of a Haitian American family that demonstrates the process of "culture swapping" through the use of consumer goods to move between two different cultural identities. These identities are involved in negotiating relations between the sending and the host cultures.

619.   Pierre-Pierre, Garry. "Haitian Refugees Find Welcome Wears Thin." *The New York Times* (6 March 1993): 26. Sect. A, Col.1. How a perceived decline in support from friends and relatives was affecting Haitian refugees.

620.   Pierre-Pierre, Garry. "At Home with Edwidge Danticat: Haitian Tales, Flatbush Scenes." *The New York Times* (26 January 1995): 1. Sect.C. An interview with a Haitian female novelist whose first book deals with a young girl's account of her early years in Haiti and eventual reunion with her immigrant mother in Brooklyn, New York. The novel is illustrative of many Haitian customs and highlights the difficulties of adjusting to Brooklyn. The novelist describes how the local Haitian community aided her adjustment to New York, parental concerns about her career, and the pleasure derived from her community's Haitian ethnicity.

621.   Schiller, Nina Glick and Georges Eugene Fouron. "Terrains of Blood and Nation: Haitian Transnational Social Fields." *Ethnic and Racial Studies* 22, no. 2 (1999): 340-366. An exploration of Haiti as a transnational nation that incorporates the experiences, needs, and aspirations of its resident and expatriate citizens living in the United States. Specifically examines how family obligation and the experiences of immigration are interpreted through familial descent, linking individuals to the concept of a transnational homeland.

622.   Smith, Alanzo H. "Toward a Caring Ministry: An Investigation Into the Needs and Concerns of Divorced or Separated Persons in West Indian Churches of the Greater New York Conference of Seventh-Day Adventists." D.Min. Dissertation, Andrews University (Canada), 1988. (No Summary available in *Dissertation Abstracts International.*)

623.   Soto, Maria. "West Indian Child Fostering: Its Role in Migrant Exchanges." Chap. 9 in *Caribbean Life in New York City: Sociocultural Dimensions*, edited by Constance R. Sutton and Elsa M. Chaney, 131-149. New York: Center for Migration Studies, 1987. West Indian child fostering involves temporary child rearing by relatives yet maintains biological parent-child ties. Since most West Indian immigrants to New York City were young women in the 1970s and 1980s, fostering maintained links with the home society through children and surrogate parents left behind. This resulted in an interchange involving immigrant parent, fosterer (in home societies), and children (both as Caribbean and New York City residents).

624.   Thrasher, Shirley Patricia. "Ethnographic Interviews with West Indian Families and a Workshop for Practitioners." D.S.W. Dissertation, City University of New York, 1988. Studies the cultural distinctiveness of parent-child relations among West Indians based on family interviews in Brooklyn, New York. Among other things, the role of the extended family, the inculcation of respect, and a strong value placed on education characterize parent-child relations in this immigrant setting.

625.   Thrasher, Shirley [Patricia], and Gary Anderson. "The West Indian Family: Treatment Challenges." *Social Casework* 69 (1988): 171-176. Explores the immigration and adjustment patterns of a group of West Indian immigrants

being counseled by a Brooklyn, New York agency that deals with child abuse, neglect, and foster care. Includes an examination of the role of the extended family, child supervision and discipline, and the tendency to seek professional help.

Chapter 7

Health Care

701.   "Anthropology and AIDS." *Medical Anthropology Quarterly (New Series)* 17 (1986): 31-38. Includes a section by Steven R. Nachman and Ginette Dreyfus who detail the damage done to Haitians in the United States by being identified as an AIDS [Acquired Immune Deficiency Syndrome] risk category and the desperate plight of Haitian AIDS patients in South Florida.

702.   Baptiste, David A. Jr., et al. "Clinical Practice with Caribbean Immigrant Families in the United States: The Intersection of Emigration, Immigration, Culture, and Race." In *Caribbean Families; Diversity among Ethnic Groups*, edited by Jaipaul L. Roopnarine and Janet Brown, 275-303. Norwood, New Jersey: Ablex Publishing Corp., 1997. Describes and discusses the dynamics and structure of English-speaking Caribbean immigrant families, including those from Belize and Guyana. Deals with issues and strategies specific to psychological therapy with all members of these families. The need to understand the structure of Caribbean families is stressed as well as the need to engage the entire family in the treatment process.

703.   Brice-Baker, Janet. "West Indian Women of Color: The Jamaican Woman." In *Women of Color: Integrating Ethnic and Gender Identities in Psychotherapy*, edited by Lillian Comas-Diaz et al., 139-160. New York: Guilford Press, 1994. This study of Jamaican-American women presents relevant historical, sociological, and psychological information about these immigrants. Clinical cases are used to illustrate certain points.   The reasons for and objectives of immigration are also examined.

704.   Canton, Denise S. "Cultural Readjustment, Coping Strategies and Mental Health Status of West Indians Residing in a United States Metropolitan Area." D.N.SC. Dissertation, Catholic University of America (Washington,

D.C.), 1984. Based on cultural adjustment and coping questionnaires and a mental health index, West Indians surveyed indicated a greater use of problem oriented strategies as opposed to the use of affective emotional behaviors in cultural adjustment. The researcher demonstrates that the use of affective coping mechanisms increases the risk of mental health problems. Further analysis indicates categories of immigrants at risk for mental problems.

705.   Chavkin, Wendy, and Carey Busner. "Reproductive Health: Caribbean Women in New York City, 1980-1984." *International Migration Review* 21 (1987): 609-625. A comparative statistical analysis of risk-factor prevalence and reproductive outcomes of non-Hispanic Caribbean women and other ethnic groups in New York City. Tables and charts organized by mothers' birthplace help illustrate such data as percentage of single live births, proportion of mothers receiving no prenatal care, low birthweight, and infant mortality. Draws no causal relationship between immigrant status and reproductive health.

706.   Chi, Peter S. K. "Health Care and Health Status of Migrant Farmworkers in New York State." *Migration Today* 8, no. 1 (1985): 39-44. Presents the results of a migrant health study conducted in Wayne County, New York in 1982. One of the three migrant groups studied consisted primarily of immigrants from Haiti and Jamaica. Survey data indicating a low level of medical utilization led to a call for employer-sponsored health care for migrant laborers.

707.   Ciesielski, S., et al. "The Seroprevalence of Cysticercosis, Malaria, and Trypanosoma-Cruzi among North Carolina Migrant Farmworkers." *Public Health Reports* 108, no. 6 (1993): 736-741. A screening for the presence of intestinal parasites and active malaria among Hispanic and Haitian migrant farmworkers in eastern North Carolina and a study of the related-maladies' prevalence. A small but significant number of the farmworkers were infected with the medical problems under consideration.

708.   Dacosta-Bagot, Patricia A. "Culture Change, Ethnicity and ociocultural Context: Acculturative Stress among Jamaican Immigrants." Ph.D. Dissertation, University of California (Los Angeles), 1985. Identified predictors of psychological health in a sample of adult Jamaican immigrant residents of Southern California. Predictor variables examined were culture change, ethnic identity, and support resources. Psychological status varied the greatest when culture change was measured in terms of social role stresses such as marital status, employment, or being a student. Support resources were the least related to the status of psychological health.

709.   Divale, William. "Cold Symptoms and Emotional Dissatisfaction among Rural Urban and Culturally Diverse High School Students." *Cross-Cultural Research* 29, no. 1 (1995): 27-47. Tested the relationship between individual emotional states and the immune system's ability to prevent common colds among high school students in Queens, New York and Rutland, Vermont. Analysis indicated that West Indian students registered greater emotional satisfaction than did students from other cultures and that African Americans and West Indians had fewer cold symptoms than did students of European or Hispanic background.

710.   Dubois, Laurent. "A Spoonful of Blood: Haitians, Racism and AIDS." *Science as Culture* 88, no. 26 (1996): 7-43. Discusses the North American stereotypes of Haiti, its people, and the voodoo religion. These stereotypes were reinforced in the 1980s when it was widely reported in the United States that Haitians were the source of the AIDS epidemic. Maintains that AIDS-related prejudices worsened as evidenced by United States immigration policies regarding Haitians suspected of carrying AIDS.

711.   Eaton, William W. "Mental Health in Mariel Cubans and Haitian Boat People." *International Migration Review* 26, no. 4 (1992): 1395-1415. A statistical analysis of a mental health survey of Mariel Cuban and Haitian immigrants who arrived in South Florida in 1980. The Haitians' lack of legal refugee status increased their likelihood of economic hardship and, therefore, heightened the expectation of mental health stresses. However, the socio-demographics of these two groups indicated a higher prevalence of mental disorder among the Cubans. The process of immigration itself did not increase the risk of mental disorders.

712.   Farmer, Paul and Jim Y. Kim. "Anthropology, Accountability, and the Prevention of AIDS." *Journal of Sex Research* 28, no. 2 (1991): 203-221. An examination of the belief that AIDS originated in Haiti and how this belief affected Haitians living in North America and complicated attempts to prevent AIDS among Haitian Americans.

713.   Fruchter, Rachel G. and Nayeri Kamran. "Cervix and Breast Cancer Incidence in Immigrant Caribbean Women." *American Journal of Public Health* 80 (June) (1990): 722-724. A comparative study of the incidence of two major types of cancer among native black and immigrant Caribbean women in Brooklyn, New York.

714.   Gopaul-McNicol, Sharon-Ann [Arlene]. "Caribbean Families Social and Emotional Problems." *Journal of Social Distress and the Homeless* 7, no. 1 (1998): 55-73. Examines the psychiatric needs of immigrant families from the English-speaking Caribbean in New York State. The issues discussed include the concept of mental illness, mental illness risk factors, psychopathological disorders, assessment, and treatment.

715.   Gordon, Antonio M. Jr. "Caribbean Basin Refugees: The Impact on Health in South Florida." *Journal of the Florida Medical Association* 69, no. 7 (1982): 523-527. A medical doctor describes the impact of recent refugees who arrived via the Mariel Cuban boatlift and Haiti on the public health and health care system in South Florida in the early 1980s. Brief discussions of health issues in the sending countries indicate an impact on refugee health in Florida. One example is the high rate of tuberculosis among Haitian refugees.

716.   Green, Charles. "Culture, Health Care and the New Caribbean Immigrants: Implications for New Health Policy and Planning." *Migration Today* 12, no. 4-5 (1984): 25-29. Discusses such West Indian cultural orientations as language and language patterns, belief in folk therapies, nutrition, and dietary habits as they relate to health problems and interactivity with medical professionals of post-1965 West Indian immigrants to New York City. Stresses the need for policy changes to ensure that health practitioners gain understanding and sensitivity to these orientations.

717.   Habenstreit, Barbara. "A Comparative Study of Health Care Behavior among Three Black Ethnic Groups." Ph.D. Dissertation, New School for Social Research (New York City), 1988. Compares health related behavior among low-income immigrant women from Haiti, the English-speaking Caribbean, and indigenous black American women living in Brooklyn, New York. Explores the interplay of cultural and socioeconomic factors associated with disease rates and responses to diagnosis. Gynecological problems and breast cancer are the main issues of focus.

718.   Habenstreit, Barbara. "Health Care Patterns of Non-Urgent Patients in an Inner City Emergency Room." *New York State Journal of Medicine* (1986): 517-521. Studies of emergency room usage at a publicly funded hospital, in a predominantly black and Hispanic section of Brooklyn, New York, indicated that only 10% of the visits were for true emergencies. Caribbean immigrants were significant consumers of this non-emergency care. A random survey of patients yielded statistics on emergency room use by ethnic group and United States vs. foreign-born patients.

719.   Hiscox, Anna. "The Art of West Indian Clients: Art Therapy as Nonverbal Modality." *Art Therapy: Journal of the American Art Therapy Association* 12, no. 2 (1995): 129-131. Maintains that culturally sensitive therapists must understand the bond among blacks of various ethnic backgrounds. Discusses major distinctions between African Americans and black West Indian clients in family relationships, language usage, and the importance of religion.

720.   Honey, Ellen. "AIDS and the Inner City: Critical Issues." *Social Casework* 69 (1988): 365-370. Considers issues surrounding AIDS unique to black and Latino inner city residents of New York City. Among the conclusions are that AIDS-related education has not been culturally relevant to the values, norms, and jargon of West Indians or other inner city residents of color.

721.   Johnson, Creola. "Quarantining HIV-Infected Haitians: United States Violations of International Law at Guantanamo Bay." *Howard Law Journal* 37 (Winter) (1994): 305-331. An examination of the legality of United States detention of HIV-positive Haitian refugees under international and American municipal law.

722.   Kleinman, Paula H., and Irving F. Lukoff. "Ethnic Differences in Factors Related to Drug Use." *Journal of Health and Social Behavior* 19 (1978): 190-199. Studies the ethnic differences in rates and patterns of the use of illicit drugs among inner-city American blacks, whites, and West Indians of British Commonwealth background. Interviews indicate that peer influences are much less powerful in West Indian than in American black or white drug use.

723.   Laguerre, Michel S. "Haitian Americans." Chap. 3 in *Ethnicity and Medical Care*, edited by Alan Harwood, 172-210. Cambridge, Mass.: Harvard University Press, 1981. Studies health behavior of primarily lower income Haitian immigrants in New York City. Reports on culturally related disease factors and the most prevalent diseases. Haitian concepts of disease and illness view the origins of illnesses as being either supernatural or natural. Various non-mainstream illness strategies, including voodoo faith healers, were tried before seeking a physician. Cultural conflicts, language and other communication problems, and patient expectations complicated encounters with mainstream medicine.

724.   Lang, Sandra. "Coping Strategies among Culturally Diverse Inmates." Ph.D. Dissertation, Miami Inst. of Psychology of the Caribbean Center for Advanced Studies (Miami, Fla.), 1995. Explored the coping strategies of cultur-

ally diverse prison inmates (American, Colombian, Jamaican, and Nigerian born). Four inventories and a demographic questionnaire were administered to the inmates. The Jamaicans appeared to experience the most stress.

725.   Mason, Marco Antonio. "The Development of a Framework for Health Care Advocacy on Behalf of Caribbean Immigrants." D.S.W. Dissertation, City University of New York, 1984. Based on the researcher's development of a health care advocacy organization directed toward Caribbean immigrants in New York City. Concludes that undocumented alien status creates significant health related stress. This conclusion led to the identification of needed health care program enhancements, to meet the needs of Caribbean immigrants.

726.   Matthews, Lear. "Social Workers' Knowledge of Client Culture and Its Use in Mental Health Care of English-Speaking Caribbean Immigrants." D.S.W. Dissertation, City University of New York, 1994. A study of "psychiatric social workers' knowledge of English-speaking Caribbean culture and the ways in which that knowledge is utilized in mental health care."

727.   Morrow, Robert D. "Immigration, Refugee and Generation Status as Related to Behavioral Disorders." In *Multicultural Issues in the Education of Students with Behavioral Disorders*, edited by Reece L. Peterson et al., 196-207. Cambridge, Mass: Brookline Books, Inc., 1994. Discusses migration patterns of various groups, including blacks that have settled in the United States. Describes potential adjustment problems of immigrants and refugees and the implications of this information for those working with behaviorally disordered children of these groups. Covers such problems as depression and post-traumatic stress disorder.

728.   Portes, Alejandro, et al. "Mental Illness and Help-Seeking Behavior among Mariel Cuban and Haitian Refugees in South Florida." *Journal of Health and Social Behavior* 33 (1992): 283-298. A statistical analysis of the differences in psychopathology and the use of mental health services by Haitians seeking refugee status and Cuban refugees in South Florida in 1980-81. Refugee background information includes means of exit from the Caribbean and reception in the United States by relatives and private and government agencies, as well cultural affinity to respective Florida ethnic communities. Includes data on six psychological disorders of these and other ethnic/nationality groups and indicators of help-seeking behavior of Cubans and Haitians.

729.   Robinson, Arnette D. "Attitudes toward the Elderly among Nursing Home Aides: A Factor Analytic Study." *Gerontology and Geriatrics Education*

14, no. 2 (1993): 21-32. "Identified the attitude dimensions employed by nursing home aides with respect to elderly nursing home residents" in the New York City metropolitan area. The aides assessed were African American and Caribbean blacks (including Haitians). Identified the salient attitude dimensions along which aides differed.

730.   Roumain, Maryse-Noel. "Accessing Mental Health and Development Disabilities Services: Some Haitian Issues and Concerns." *Migration World Magazine* 17, no. 2 (1989): 34-39. Studies the problems that arise from the "differences between the structure of services and the health-seeking patterns of minorities," primarily Haitians in New York City.

731.   Ruducha, Jenny. *Migrant Child Health: The Role of Social, Cultural, and Economic Factors.* 1994. ERIC, ED 382 435. Examines differences in measures of health status and health services utilization among migrant and non-immigrant children in Virginia, Delaware, and Maryland. The groups studied were Mexican Americans, Haitians, and whites. Highlighted are differences in family socio-economic conditions, literacy, and health insurance.

732.   Scott, Clarissa S. "Health and Healing Practices among Five Ethnic Groups in Miami, Florida." *Public Health Reports* 89, no. 6 (1974): 524-532. Anthropological/sociological studies of the health care practices of Bahamians, Haitians, southern American blacks, Cubans, and Puerto Ricans in Miami, Florida. All groups attributed "certain symptoms and conditions to social and interpersonal conflict" and the supernatural. Haitians tended to treat illness first with herbs and home remedies, then with religious ("Vodoun") healers or prayer. All groups used different therapies serially or concurrently and failed to rely solely on scientific medicine.

733.   Seabrooks, Patricia Ann Johnson. "Social Supports of Older Haitians in Port-au-Prince and Miami: Effects on Health Practices and Perceived Health Status." D.N.S. Dissertation, University of California, San Francisco, 1992. Explores the impact of the preference of older ethnic minorities to use informal social support networks for health care. Considers the related special problems faced by older Haitian immigrants in Miami, Florida. Compares the use of social support networks and the health-seeking practices of older Haitians in Miami, Florida with those in Port-au-Prince, Haiti.

734.   Thrasher, Shirley P. "Psychodynamic Therapy and Culture in the Treatment of Incest of a West Indian Immigrant." *Journal of Child Sexual Abuse*

3, no. 1 (1994): 37-52. Explores the treatment of an adult West Indian female who was sexually abused both as a child and as an adolescent. Such studies add to a knowledge base of culturally specific treatment techniques.

735.   Todd, Caron Thalia. "Difference in Rates of Reported Disease among Regional Subgroups of the Black Population in Harlem." Ph.D. Dissertation, Columbia University (New York City), 1988. Investigates the differences among black regional subgroups in the Harlem population from 1967 to 1970. Includes the finding that West Indian immigrants reported fewer health problems than other groups and puts forth possible cultural and physical reasons for this difference.

736.   Weatherby, Norman L., et al. "Immigration and HIV among Migrant Workers in Rural Southern Florida." *Journal of Drug Issues* 27, no. 1 (Winter) (1997): 155-173. A study of HIV positive status among migrant workers who were drug users and their sexual partners in rural South Florida. Among the groups studied were Caribbean blacks. Race/ethnicity and age, not current sexual activity, were most highly associated with HIV positive status.

737.   Welte, John W., and Grace M. Barnes. "Alcohol Use Among Adolescent Minority Groups." *Journal of Studies on Alcohol* 48, no. 4 (1987): 329-336. Surveys of 7th-12th grade students in New York State indicated that native black and West Indian students had the lowest per capita use of alcohol and the lowest illicit drug use among other ethnic or racial groups. Statistics indicate the relationship between the percentage of students who drink and the percentage of heavy drinkers based on gender and racial/ethnic group.

738.   Welte, John W., and Grace M. Barnes. "Youthful Smoking: Patterns and Relationships to Alcohol and Other Drug Use." *Journal of Adolescence* 10 (1987): 327-340. Surveyed the smoking habits of high school students in public and private schools of New York State. One table detailing smoking behavior by sex, ethnicity, and age indicated that West Indians smoked less than other ethnic groups surveyed.

Chapter 8

Immigration and Settlement Patterns

801.   Allman, James. "Haitian Migration: Thirty Years Assessed." *Migration Today* 10, no. 1 (1982): 7-12. An analysis of Haitian migration, between 1950 and 1980, to the United States, the Dominican Republic and the Bahamas. With a 1980 estimated Haitian population of 450,000, the United States was the most important receiving country. A statistical table illustrates this yearly flow by type of visa.

802.   Anderson, Jervis. "A Reporter at Large: The Haitians of New York." *The New Yorker* 51 (31 March) (1975): 50-75. The early 1970s Haitian community in New York City is said to be the city's most isolated immigrant group and, therefore, unable to obtain needed services. Estimates the city's total Haitian population and describes the group's residential neighborhoods in Manhattan, Brooklyn, and Queens. The roles of religion, the arts, and social gatherings are also explored. Describes how immigration, housing, employment, and other problems are addressed by several Haitian community organizations. Also discusses the role of local Haitian newspapers, including *Haiti Observateur*, and a short-wave radio station.

803.   Bach, Robert L. "Caribbean Migration: Causes and Consequences." *Migration Today* 10, no. 5 (1982): 6-13. Focuses on the 1970s and outlines some of the causal factors of migration from the West Indies: "recruitment by labor and government employers, escape from violence or coercion, family reunification, and a migrant ideology among the people."

804.   Borge, Michelle. "Haitian Refugees: (Haiti's) Missing Persons." *Migration Today* 12, no. 4 (1979): 9-11. Considers the fate of Haitians fleeing the Duvalier regimes and attempting to claim political refugee status in the United States. The United States claim that the Haitians were only economic

refugees was supported by the report of a United States State Dept. study team sent to Haiti. Challenges the study team's methods and results.

805.   Boswell, Thomas D. "The New Haitian Diaspora: Florida's Most Recent Residents." *Caribbean Review* 11 (Winter) (1982): 18-21. In late 1972, Haitian migration patterns shifted dramatically from arrival in New York City, often via the Bahamas, to arrival in South Florida directly from Haiti. Undocumented Haitian boat people began to flow directly to Florida in barely sea-worthy vessels. Includes demographic data on Haitians in South Florida, during the late 1970s. Discusses immigrants' regional origins in Haiti, settlement patterns in South Florida, and Haitian public school enrollment in Dade County, Florida.

806.   Brimelow, Peter. "Time to Rethink Immigration? The Decline of the Americanization of Immigrants." *National Review* 44 (22 June) (1992): 30-42+. Immigration from the English speaking Caribbean increased by a factor of five during the 1960s, with some 220,000 West Indians living in the New York City area by 1973. Jamaican immigrants to the United States between 1951 and 1980 constituted a tenth of the island nation's population.

807.   Broyles, William. "Promise Of America." *U.S. News & World Report* 100 (7 July 1986): 25-30. Immigrant groups are having a revitalizing impact on certain New York City neighborhoods, including Haitians in parts of Brooklyn and Queens. New York City is seen as the classic laboratory for the three-generation immigrant experience.

808.   Bryce-Laporte, Roy S. ed. "Caribbean Immigration to the United States." RIIES Occasional Papers No. 1. Washington, DC: Smithsonian Institution, 1983. ERIC, ED 283 890. Includes 12 research papers on Caribbean immigration to the United States. The papers cover such topics as the United States role in Caribbean immigration; underdevelopment and migration; economic status of immigrants; Haitians in Boston; West Indians in Los Angeles; return migration, and the migration of professionals.

809.   Bryce-Laporte, Roy S. "The Immigration of Caribbean People to the U.S.: Some Comments." *Kroeber Anthropological Society Papers*, no. 65-66 (1986): 25-34. Identifies early Caribbean individual and group (transported slaves') contributors to America's development. This migratory movement was both direct and indirect, influenced by United States money, technology, and political power. Twentieth century immigrants played significant roles on Southern farms and in Northern cities. Significant contributors of this second group are identified and the economic characteristics of 1980s West Indian immigrants are discussed.

810.   Bryce-Laporte, Roy S. "Visibility of the New Immigrants." *Society* 14 , no. 6 (1977): 18-22. Legal immigration to the United States between 1965 and

1977 is discussed with an emphasis on immigration from Southeast Asia, Latin America, and the Caribbean. Also examines the impact of the Immigration Act of 1965, which helped spur this movement and the immigrants' impact on American daily life and culture.

811.   Bryce-Laporte, Roy S. "Voluntary Immigration and Continuing Encounters between Blacks: The Post-Quincentary Challenge." *Annals of the American Academy of Political and Social Science* 530 (1993): 28-41. Continued human migration is seen to be a major dynamic resulting from the American encounters of Christopher Columbus and voluntary black migration to the United States, a major element of that dynamic. Contributions of Caribbean immigrants to the life of black New York City in the 1920s and 1930s are noted, along with a historical survey of relevant United States immigration policy. With the 1965 United States Immigration Act, black Caribbean immigrants became more visible, adding diversifying elements of ethnicity and nationality to the United States black population and the realization of pan-Caribbeanism in America's urban areas.

812.   Buchanan, Susan H. "Profile of a Haitian Migrant Woman." Chap. 7 in *Female Immigrants to the United States: Caribbean, Latin American, and African Experiences*, edited by Delores M. Mortimer and Roy S. Bryce-Laporte, 112-142. RIIES Occasional Papers, No. 2. Washington, D.C.: Smithsonian Institution, 1981. ERIC, ED 278 721. Interviews were used to create a composite picture of Haitian female adaptation to New York City. The profile explores the incorporation of these arrivals into the local Haitian community, their employment opportunities, and their role in assisting family members locally and in Haiti, as well as their local family and community relationships. Includes an overview of post-1956 Haitian immigration to the United States and New York City.

813.   Buchanan, Susan Huelsebusch. "Scattered Seeds: The Meaning of the Migration for Haitians in New York City." Ph.D. Dissertation, New York University, 1980. Explores the cultural meaning of Haitian migration to New York City and the effect a unique Haitian culture has on the collective action of these immigrants. Conflicts among Haitians over the use of language in a Brooklyn Catholic church is the nexus for exploring cultural ramifications of Haitian migration to New York City. Finally, Haitians are seen as social actors shaping their own political reality.

814.   Burns, Allan F. *Ethnic Transformations in Late-Twentieth-Century Florida*. Philadelphia: Temple University Press, 1993. Explores Florida's twentieth-century history of migrations and how its multicultural nature has changed dramatically since 1960. While Cubans and other Hispanics make up a large part of this cultural mix, Haitians and Jamaicans now have a major demographic impact on South Florida.

815.   Chaney, Elsa M. "The Context of Caribbean Migration." Chap. 1 in *Caribbean Life in New York City: Sociocultural Dimensions*, edited by Constance M. Sutton and Elsa M. Chaney, 3-13. New York: Center for Migration Studies, 1987. New York City and the Caribbean interact in a continuous circular exchange of ideas, goods, culture, and people that influence the West Indian immigrant experience and the overall life of the city. Strong immigrant ties to home societies make it necessary to understand the factors that impel immigration to New York City. Dependency and a heritage of migration are two major "push" factors explored during four major periods of Caribbean migration. Related immigration statistics are included for 1966-1975.

816.   "Coming North: Latino and Caribbean Immigration." *NACLA Report on the Americas* 26 (July) (1992): 13-49. Discusses the motivation for migration, "migrant distinctions and experience in the [United States], and United States immigration policy as it relates to the Mexican border, Haitians, and Latino farmworkers."

817.   Conway, Denis. "Emigration to North America: The Continuing Option for the Caribbean." *Caribbean Affairs* 3 (April/June) (1990): 109-119. An examination of Caribbean demographic trends from the 1950s through the 1980s reflects the increase in Caribbean migration to Canada and the United States. This trend is found to have resulted from both changes in North American immigration policies and political/economic changes in the Caribbean.

818.   DeWind, Josh. "Alien Justice: The Exclusion of Haitian Refugees." *Journal of Social Issues* 46, no. 1 (1990): 121-132. Related international conventions support the claim that the United States systematically denied procedural justice to Haitian asylum seekers. The United States government's late 1970s "Haitian Program" denied due process and expedited the expulsion of Haitians. This was followed by the 1981 policy of interdicting Haitian boat people on the high seas and returning them to Haiti. Haitian refugees were seen as a threat to United States domestic and various cold war foreign policy interests. Haitians were denied fair adjudication of their asylum claims because the relevant United States agencies were primarily concerned with national security interests.

819.   De Witt, Karen. "Immigrants Look Outside New York for Better Life." *The New York Times* (4 September 1990): 3. Sect.B, Col.1. Some Caribbean residents of New York City comment that changes in United States immigration laws have enabled the immigration of West Indians to the United States who lack traditional values of stability. The influence of Jamaican gang members in Harlem and Brooklyn is cited as an example of this observation. An increasing number of these observers have decided to leave New York City.

820.   Dreyfuss, Joel. "The Invisible Immigrants." *The New York Times* (23 May 1993): Sect.6, Pg.20, Col. 1. A successful Haitian immigrant explores the

socioeconomic characteristics of his contemporaries who have progressed in New York City. Social problems encountered by some Haitians and self-help efforts are also discussed.

821.   Duany, Jorge. "Beyond the Safety Valve: Recent Trends in Caribbean Migration." *Social and Economic Studies* 43, no. 1 (1994): 95-122. Divides the Caribbean's emigration history into six major periods beginning with Haitian exile movements to the United States and other countries, from 1791 to 1838. The post-1940s and post-1960s movement to the United States is analyzed as part of a fifth period. The demographic and socioeconomic nature (including labor market impact) of West Indian immigration to the United States during the 1980s and 1990s is emphasized in exploring the sixth period. Also assessed are the impact of these movements on Caribbean societies and the theory of migration as a safety valve.

822.   Eddie, David. "Refugees From Unrest: Central American and Caribbean Immigrants in the United States (Includes Related Information)." *Scholastic Update (Teacher's Edition)* 120 (11 March 1988): 22-23. New York City and Miami, Florida are discussed as primary goals for Haitian immigrants since the 1960s.

823.   Edmonds, Arlene. "The African Caribbean Community." *Philadelphia Tribune* (26 January) 112 , no. 112 (Supplement) (1996): 18-19. Reports on Philadelphia's West Indian heritage and growing West Indian population. Notes the settlement patterns of West Indian migrants since 1880. Cooperation with African Americans is described, as well as changed attitudes toward Jamaicans since 1990. Local ethnic organizations are also described.

824.   Elwell, Patricia J. and Charles B. Keely. "Haitian and Dominican Undocumented Aliens in New York City: A Preliminary Report." *Migration Today* 5, no. 5 (1977): 5-9. Presents a statistical look at Haitian and Dominican undocumented immigrants, including such factors as immigrant age by national origin and gender, educational attainment, duration of United States residence, and language skills. Other findings deal with marital status, family structure, visa abuse, occupational distribution, and social service participation.

825.   Feen, Richard H. "The Never Ending Story: The Haitian Boat People." *Migration World Magazine* 21, no. 1 (1993): 13-15. A report on the continuing effort of people to flee political/economic turmoil in Haiti and seek refuge in the United States in the early 1990s. Changing United States policies and court challenges were reflected in interdiction at sea, detention in offshore camps, and forced repatriation of refugees.

826.   Fernandez-Kelly, M. Patricia and Richard Schauffler. "Divided Fates: Immigrant Children in a Restructured U.S. Economy." *International Migration Review* 28, no. 28 (1994): 662-689. Compares segmented assimilation of second

generation immigrant children, including Haitians in South Florida, as affected by factors such as physical location and reception by the host society. Successful Haitians have emphasized their nationality and religions to avoid the stigma placed on native black Americans and, therefore, have avoided assimilation. Other Haitians have been negatively impacted by Miami's impoverished black neighborhoods. Various tables compare ethnic group school performance, friendship networks, perceptions of discrimination, and socioeconomic status.

827.   Foner, Nancy. "Jamaicans in New York City." *Migration Today* 12, no. 3 (1984): 6-12. Analyzes the flow of Jamaicans to New York City from 1967 through 1979. With women outnumbering men, emigrants saw particular economic, educational, and social benefits to settling in New York City. Negative aspects of life in the city, such as crime and discrimination, are also explored as they relate to future plans for these immigrants.

828.   Frankenhoff, Charles A. "Cuban, Haitian Refugees in Miami: Public Policy Needs for Growth from Welfare to Mainstream." *Migration Today* 13, no. 3 (1985): 6-13. Examines the public policy needs (e.g., health, housing, and education) for Cuban and Haitian refugees in Dade County (Miami), Florida. Argues the importance of identifying refugee problems from the refugee's point of view as well as the view of service professionals.

829.   French, Howard W. "Caribbean Exodus: U.S. Is Constant Magnet." *The New York Times* (6 May 1992): 1. Sect.A, Col.2. Old communities are being revitalized and new ones created in New York and New Jersey by the influx of immigrants from the Caribbean.

830.   Garcia, John A. "Caribbean Migration to the Mainland: A Review of Adaptive Experiences." *Annals of the American Academy of Political and Social Science* 487 (1986): 114-125. Compares the societal incorporation processes of English-speaking West Indians, Haitians, and Dominicans in New York City and the Southeastern United States as a three-phase process. Government policy, ethnocentrism, and racism are said to prevent Haitians from succeeding in the adaptation phase of the process. The success of West Indian New Yorkers, compared with African Americans and Haitians, indicated better societal incorporation.

831.   Gordon, Monica. "In Search of the Means to a Better Life: Caribbean Migration to the United States." Paper Presented at the Five College Black Studies Seminar Series. Amherst, Mass., (10 March), 1982. ERIC, ED 228 343. Concludes that Caribbean migration to the United States resulted primarily from American investments in the region. As related economic opportunities declined in the Caribbean, migrants sought sanctuary in the United States. The United States is said to have benefited from the influx of these workers. While some immigrants achieved economically, others were pushed to the economic underclass.

832.   "The Haitian Crisis: A Catholic Response." *Migration World Magazine* 20, no. 1 (1991): 25-28. A Catholic priest (based in Miami, Florida) details the work of a church migration and refugee service. His work to secure favorable federal legislation, resettlement, legal services, and pastoral service is described. Refugees are seen as a tool of foreign policy and the church agency as an advocate of refugee needs.

833.   Helton, Arthur C. "The United States Government Program of Intercepting and Forcibly Returning Haitian Boat People to Haiti: Policy Implications and Prospects." *New York Law School Journal of Human Rights* 10 (Spring) (1993): 325-349. Explores the United States government's policy, introduced in 1981, to intercept at sea and forcibly return potential American Haitian refugees to their homeland. Discusses the four phases of implementing the program, its departure from accepted international practice, and race as a factor in United States immigration and refugee policy.

834.   Helton, Arthur C. "United States Refugee Policy: African and Caribbean Effects." *TransAfrica Forum* 9, no. 2 (1992): 93-102. Considers the history of United States immigration and refugee policies, finding that the 1980s/1990s refugee policies were essentially racially based. Views the forcible detention and repatriation of Haitian asylum seekers as an example of this racial policy. Calls for reform in the Haitian interdiction program.

835.   Hinds, Lester. "200 Caribbean Nationals Deported Since January from New York Area." *New York Amsterdam News* (9 May 1992): Pg.9, Col.1. Covers the deportation of Caribbean nationals in 1992 from New York City primarily on the basis of convictions involving illegal drugs.

836.   Hoh, Harold Hongju. "The Haitian Refugee Litigation: A Case Study in Transnational Public Law Litigation." *Maryland Journal of International Law and Trade* 18 (Spring) (1994): 1-20. Deals with a lawsuit filed in November, 1991 by the Haitian Refugee Center against the United States Immigration and Naturalization Service in Florida, challenging the government's practice of returning screened out Haitians.

837.   Houston, Marion F., et al. "Female Predominance in Immigration to the United States Since 1930: A First Look." *International Migration Review* 18, no. 4 (1984): 908-963. Analyzes causes and effects of the predominance of females in the post-1930 immigration flow to the United States. Valuable statistical tables for the period 1972-1979, verifying this trend for the West Indies, include origin of female immigrants to the United States, countries sending the largest number of female immigrants, and states receiving the largest number of female immigrants.

838.   Hughes, Joyce A., and Linda R. Crane. "Haitians: Seeking Refuge in the United States." *Georgetown Immigration Law Journal* 7 (December) (1993):

747-815. Explores American policy concerning Haitian refugees, since the 1970s, based on an agreement with the Haitian government. That agreement permitted the interdiction (on the high seas) and repatriation of Haitians seeking refuge in the United States. Hostility toward Haitians was demonstrated by United States administrative and court decisions and government treatment of Haitians when compared to Cubans, Salvadorans, and Chinese. Some 50,000 Haitians sought political asylum in the United States between 1972 and 1980, but only 25 succeeded.

839.   "Immigrants and Refugees: The Caribbean and South Florida." Occasional Papers Series, Dialogues #2. Miami, Florida: Florida International University, Latin American and Caribbean Center, 1981. ERIC, ED 263 277. Includes six papers on Caribbean immigrants and refugees in South Florida. Two of these papers are: "Estimates of Haitian International Migration for the 1950-1980 Period" and "West Indian Migration: Historical Notes and Contemporary Trends."

840.   Jones-Hendrickson, S. B. "An Analysis of Immigration: St. Kitts-Nevis to the U.S. Virgin Islands." *Migration Today* 8, no. 2 (1980): 24-27. By the late 1970s, about 25 percent of the eastern Caribbean citizens in the United States Virgin Islands were from St. Kitts-Nevis. For many migrants, the United States Virgin Islands was America and affected their ability to quickly increase their incomes and other assets. Remittances, the unemployment differential, and the income differential underpin this net migration.

841.   Jorge, Antonio. "Perspectives on Recent Refugees and Immigrant Waves into South Florida." Occasional Papers Series, Dialogues #6. ERIC, ED 263 280. Includes six papers presented at a 1982 forum on Latin American and Caribbean migration to South Florida. Topics included discuss two decades of refugee and other immigrant flow; related United States refugee and immigration policy; the economic impact of this flow; and Haitian refugees in the United States.

842.   Kessner, Thomas and Betty Boyd Caroli. "I Was Afraid but More I Was Hungry: Brooklyn's West Indians." Chap. 7 in *Today's Immigrants, Their Stories: A New Look At the Newest Americans*, edited by Thomas Kessner and Betty Boyd Caroli, 185-203. New York: Oxford University Press, 1982. Notes probable reasons that Brooklyn had New York City's largest West Indian Community by the late 1970s. Discusses the estrangement between West Indian blacks and native black Americans within the context of West Indian migration to New York City since 1900. One among several reasons explored for significant Jamaican migration (and especially female migration) to New York is United States immigration policies, although these policies are seen as establishing a form of indentured household labor for thousands of Jamaican women. Haitian migration to the United States, in the late 1960s and 70s, and resulting settlement and occupational patterns in New York City are also explored.

843.   Klopner, Michele Anne Cuvilly. "A Composite Profile of Haitian Immigrants in the United States Based on a Community Needs Assessment." Ph.D. Dissertation, Rutgers the State University of New Jersey (New Brunswick, N.J.), 1985. Presents a structured interview design to assess the needs of legal and undocumented Haitian immigrants in areas such as health care, employment, education, and regularization of alien status.

844.   Kraly, Ellen P. "United States Immigration Policy and the Immigrant Populations of New York." Chap. 2 in *New Immigrants in New York*, edited by Nancy Foner, 35-78. New York: Columbia University Press, 1987. As of 1980, twelve percent of all foreign-born and fifty percent of most West Indian residents of the United States lived in New York City. The history of United States immigration policy, and the interrelationship of post-1965 patterns of immigration flow, is discussed in this analysis of New York City's status as a primary destination for immigrants. The dynamics of this influx on the city's overall ethnic diversity and the focused patterns of neighborhood residence are analyzed and reflected in valuable statistical tables.

845.   Laguerre, Michel S. *American Odyssey: Haitians in New York City.* Ithaca, N.Y.: Cornell University Press, 1984. Expands on an earlier article, "The Haitian Niche in New York City," with a broader look at Haitian socioeconomic adaptation to certain neighborhoods in Brooklyn, Queens, and Manhattan in the 1970s. Discussion of the migration process and settlement in New York is enhanced with three 1970 maps designating Haitian households by borough. Daily life is explored through family organization, employment, the economics of credit associations, health beliefs and practices, and ethnic political culture.

846.   Laguerre, Michel S. *Disasporic Citizenship: Haitian Americans in Transnational America.* New York: St. Martin's Press, 1997. Provides a concise history of the Haitian Diaspora in the United States during the 19th century but concentrates on the late 20th century and specifically the Haitian community in New York City. It uses a transnational perspective in describing the adaptation of Haitian-Americans and their border-crossing behavior to maintain connections with Haiti. Includes valuable statistical appendices.

847.   Laguerre, Michel S. "The Haitian Niche in New York City." *Migration Today* 7, no. 4 (September) (1979): 12-18. A socioeconomic analysis of the Haitian community in various New York City neighborhoods during the 1970s. The role of Catholic and Protestant churches, social gatherings, soccer, and community theatre are among the topics discussed. In the ongoing practice of voodoo, the voodoo priest is seen as a folk healer and cult leader. Haitian students' difficulties with the education system and the role of voluntary associations are also outlined. Based on a manuscript for the author's later book *American Odyssey: Haitians in New York City.*

848.   Lawless, Robert. "Haitian Migrants and Haitian-Americans: From Invisibility into the Spotlight." *Journal of Ethnic Studies* 14 (Summer) (1986): 29-70. Examines the language, culture, religion, and assimilation of Haitian immigrants to New York and Florida in the 1970s and 1980s. Other Americans were generally ignorant of the overall size and culture of the Haitian community. This ignorance led to the misconception that Haitians were primary carriers of the HIV virus.

849.   Little, Cheryl. "United States Haitian Policy: A History of Discrimination." *New York Law School Journal of Human Rights* 10 (1993): 269-324. Concludes that the United States government flouted international law and the will of the United States Congress in denying asylum to most refugees fleeing Haiti between 1980 and 1991. Reviews how the Haitian issue was treated in the courts, the detention of Haitians seeking asylum, the disparity in the treatment of Cuban and Haitian refugees, and the United States-Haiti interdiction agreement.

850.   Lobo, Arthur Peter and Joseph J. Salvo. "Immigration to New York City in the '90s: The Saga Continues." *Migration World Magazine* 25, no. 3 (1997): 14-17. Reports on a New York City study, which documented that immigration to the city had increased significantly between 1990-1994 as compared to the 1980s. Immigration flow from the Caribbean increased thirty-three percent to the city, but only twelve- percent to the nation. West Indian nations remained among the top sending countries, although there was a decline in flows from these countries since the 1980s.

851.   Loescher, Gilburt and John Scanlan. "Human Rights, U.S. Foreign Policy, and Haitian Refugees." *Journal of Interamerican Studies and World Affairs* 26 (1984): 313-357. Argues that United States policy denying political asylum to Haitians, in the 1970s and 1980s, was based on United States foreign policy alliance with Haitian presidents against Cuba and Communism. Other potential Haitian government cooperation, including the possibility of a United States military base in Haiti, also influenced United States denial of refugee status to Haitians. From Presidents Eisenhower (1950s) to Reagan (1980s), American procedures deliberately hindered Haitian claims for asylum. These policies denied human rights abuses in Haiti as well as United States legislation and court decisions favorable to Haitian claims.

852.   Maingot, Anthony P. "Caribbean Migration as Structural Reality." Occasional Papers Series. Dialogues #13. Revised version of a paper presented to the Conference on Caribbean Migration sponsored by Georgetown University and Greater Miami United. Miami, FL, 8 December 1982. ERIC, ED 263 282. Describes Caribbean regional demographic and economic conditions impelling migration to the United States as shifting but constant. Further discusses five "pull" factors that encourage Caribbean migration to the United States.

853.   Maingot, Anthony P. "Immigration from the Caribbean Basin." Chap. 2 in *Miami Now! Immigration, Ethnicity, and Social Change*, edited by Guillermo J. Grenier and Alex Stepick, 18-40. Gainesville, Fla.: University Press of Florida, 1992. Immigrant flows from the Caribbean to the United States are calculated to exceed those from all other areas during the late 1970s and 1980s. This fact is illustrated with related statistics. Among the reasons that the United States exerts such a pull factor for Caribbean immigrants are the successes of West Indians in the United States and the existence of social-cultural enclaves in Miami, Florida and other American urban areas.

854.   Maingot, Anthony P. "The Stress Factor in Migration: A Dissenting View." *Migration Today* 13, no. 5 (1985): 26-29. Immigrants to the New York City area are cited as an example to dispute the view that stress and adaptation difficulties are constant elements of the migration experience.

855.   McCoy, Terry L. "United States Policy on Caribbean Migration: A Preliminary Study." *Revista/Review InterAmericana* 11, no. 3 (Fall) (1981): 399-417. Predicts a tightening of United States restrictions on immigration from the West Indies. Explores the conflicting domestic pressures to restrict immigration and the foreign policy goals to permit it.

856.   Miller, Jake C. *The Plight of Haitian Refugees*. New York: Praeger, 1984. Studies the impact of Haitian refugees on South Florida in the 1970s and differences in their treatment from that of other refugees to the United States. The study considered Haitians to be de facto refugees because the economic and social structure of Haiti denied them basic human rights that are identified and analyzed. Also considered were methods used by Haitians to gain entry to the United States, United States government efforts to return Haitians to Haiti, problems faced by Haitians who have settled in the United States, and strategies used to obtain more equitable treatment.

857.   Millman, Joel. "Ghetto Blasters." *Forbes* 157, no. 3 (12 February) (1996): 76-82. Reports that West Indian immigrants have caused the resurgence in home ownership in some of Brooklyn New York's black neighborhoods since 1980. These areas have been renewed after almost thirty years of middle class black American flight. Describes the human capital these immigrants bring and their resultant middle class living standards.

858.   Mitchell, Christopher. "From Policy Frontier to Policy Dilemmas: The United States and Caribbean Migration, 1960-1990." *European Review of Latin American and Caribbean Studies*, no. 52 (June) (1992): 75-89. Reviews Caribbean immigration to the United States from 1960 through the 1980s. Includes statistics on the number of immigrant and non-immigrant visas issued by the United States for five West Indian countries. The legislative and executive mechanisms of setting relevant United States immigration policy are also surveyed. West Indian migration was viewed positively by the federal gov-

ernment through the 1970s. This view changed in the late 1970s and 1980s when Haitian refugees came to be seen as economic and political liabilities.

859.   Mitchell, Christopher. "United States Policy Toward Haitian Boat People, 1972-93." *Annals of the American Academy of Political and Social Science* 534 (1994): 69-80. Reviews United States treatment of undocumented Haitian boat people who began migrating by sea to Florida in the 1970s. Strong political and economic forces in South Florida are seen as driving United States efforts to deter, then detain indefinitely, and finally intercept Haitians at sea, and return them to Haiti. Various legal and technical methods were used to prevent this migration until the early 1990s. The United States then saw this migratory pressure as a political lever to restore a democratically elected president, Jean-Bertrand Aristide, to power in Haiti.

860.   Mohl, Raymond A. "An Ethnic "Boiling Pot": Cubans and Haitians in Miami." *Journal of Ethnic Studies* 13, no. 2 (1985): 51-74. Surveys the scope and characteristics of Cuban and Haitian migration to Miami, Florida in the 1970s and early 1980s that changed the city's ethnic and racial makeup. Haitian settlement patterns, demographic characteristics, educational and work ethic and limited socioeconomic mobility are the primary topics discussed.

861.   Mortimer, Delores M., and Roy S. Bryce-Laporte, eds. "Female Immigrants to the United States: Caribbean, Latin America, and African Experiences." Washington, D.C.: Smithsonian Institution, 1981. RIIES Occasional Papers No. 2; ERIC, ED 278 721. A collection of seminar papers exploring social adjustment issues, including racism and sexism, experienced by immigrant women. Papers dealing with West Indian women explore such topics as: working class Jamaicans and migration; female Trinidadians in New York City; professional/managerial women; black immigrant women in Paule Marshall's novel *Brown Girl, Brownstones*; Haitian immigrant women; and the female Caribbean brain drain. Includes a sizable bibliography.

862.   Nossiter, Adam. "A Jamaican Way Station in the Bronx: Community of Striving Immigrants Fosters Middle-Class Values." *The New York Times* (25 October 1995): B1-B2. Chronicles two middle class Jamaican neighborhoods located in the northeastern section of the Bronx, New York. The neighborhoods have substantial single-family houses, stable families, low unemployment, and little poverty. Includes a chart that compares these neighborhoods with two Jamaican neighborhoods in Brooklyn on population, unemployment, income level, and home ownership.

863.   Palmer, Ransford W. "Illegal Migration from the Caribbean." Chap. 9 in *In Search of a Better Life: Perspectives on Migration from the Caribbean*, edited by Ransford W. Palmer, 163-174. New York: Praeger, 1990. Examines undocumented migration from the English-speaking Caribbean region (including Belize), focusing on Jamaica, from 1963 to 1986. Most of the undoc-

umented entered with temporary visas, making this a migration of the middle class and dominated by students. Statistics on undocumented Jamaicans indicate a low rate of visa violation and a high rate of apprehension.

864.   Papademetriou, Demetrios G. *New Immigrants to Brooklyn and Queens: Policy Implications, Especially with Regard to Housing.* Staten Island, New York: Center for Migration Studies of New York, Inc., 1983. Based on 1970 and 1980 United States government data, registered Caribbean alien residents of two New York City boroughs are profiled in Section 3 "Race and Ethnicity in New York" and Section 4 "The Social and Economic Adjustment of New Immigrants." Section 3 includes country of origin rankings of registered aliens in Brooklyn and in Queens for 1977 and 1980. Ethnic group distribution is also presented in charts of borough postal zip code areas and a table of borough neighborhoods.

865.   Pierre-Pierre, Garry. "Heading to Florida, Nearer the Homeland." *The New York Times* (13 July 1993): 3. Sect.B, Col.1. Crime and poverty have led many Caribbean New Yorkers to relocate to Florida. Many of these individuals had achieved financial success but despaired of the New York City environments they were exposed to. Included are 1990 United States Census figures on West Indian migration from New York to Florida as well as to Georgia and Texas for 1985-1990. Migration figures from the West Indies to New York City are also cited for the same time period.

866.   Powers, Thomas. "The Scandal of United States Immigration: The Haitian Example." *MS! [MS Magazine].* 4, no. 8 (1976): 62-83. Describes the early 1970s migration of Haitian boat people to south Florida and the refusal of the United States to recognize them as political refugees. However, careful questioning of the refugees led to clear descriptions of the political brutality of Haiti. The United States denied Haitian refugee claims, while recognizing refugees from Communist countries, for fear of the rise of a Haitian equivalent of Fidel Castro.

867.   Ricketts, Erol. "U.S. Investment and Immigration from the Caribbean." *Social Problems* 34, no. 4 (1987): 374-387. The growth in direct United States investment in the Caribbean, during the 1970s, is found to have a direct relationship to emigration from those countries to the United States

868.   Roney, Lisa S. "Amnesty for Illegal Aliens from the Caribbean: Implications for Future Immigration Flows." Chap. 8 in *In Search of a Better Life: Perspectives on Migration from the Caribbean*, edited by Ransford W. Palmer, 153-161. New York: Praeger, 1990. Discusses the participation of undocumented Caribbean immigrants in regularizing their status under the United States Immigration Reform and Control Act of 1986. Data is presented on the total number of Caribbean applicants for the legislation's two major programs: regularization of those living in undocumented status before 1982 and

special agricultural workers. Applicants are characterized by age structure, gender, national origin, and United States settlement patterns. Most special agricultural applicants were Haitians and Jamaicans.

869.   Salvo, Joseph J. "Immigration to New York City in the Post-1965 Era: Sex Selectivity and the Economic Role of Women." Chap. 3 in *The Immigration Experience in the United States: Policy Implications*, edited by Mary G. Powers and John J. Macisco Jr., 46-72. Staten Island, N.Y.: The Center for Migration Studies, 1994. Analyzes the gender composition of immigrants to New York City, concentrating on 1982-1989. Caribbean countries were among the top senders of immigrants to the city and females generally outnumbered males. Females from Central America and the Caribbean had the highest levels of employment and established niches in service occupations, leading to successive waves of immigration. Valuable statistical tables cover topics such as the percentage of female immigrants by occupation and country of origin.

870.   Schey, Peter A. "The Black Boat People Flounder on the Shoals of United States Policy." *Migration Today* 9, no. 4-5 (1981): 7-10. Argues that United States foreign policy of appeasing a repressive government in Haiti caused the United States to reject most Haitian refugee claims of asylum in the late 1970s and 1980. The United States government maintained that most of the Haitian boat people were economic and not political refugees. A policy of interdiction and refugee camps is accurately forecast.

871.   Shacknove, Andrew E. "The American Response to Haitian Refugee Migration." Ph.D. Dissertation, Yale University, (New Haven, Conn.) 1987. Examines the political, economic, and moral dimensions of the American response to Haitian refugee migration to the United States in the 1980s. Outlines a preferred concept of refugee status and principles for guiding and evaluating American refugee policy. A structural basis for this evaluation results from a discussion of the political economy of Haitian migration.

872.   Sontag, Deborah. "A City of Immigrants Is Pictured in Report." *The New York Times* (1 July 1992): 1. Sect.B, Col.2. Guyana, Haiti, and Jamaica were among the top five countries sending immigrants to New York City, based on a city agency report. This immigrant flow, from 1982 to 1989, is contrasted with the flow to the United States as a whole. Some unique characteristics of the City's Caribbean and Latin American dominated immigrant culture are also explored.

873.   Sontag, Deborah. "Study Sees Illegal Aliens in New Light." *The New York Times* (2 September 1993): 1. Sect.B, Col.2. Reports on a then recent New York City Planning Dept. study, indicating that most undocumented immigrants in New York City come from Europe, the Caribbean (especially Haiti and Jamaica), and Latin America.

874.   "Status Needs Positive Change. Report of the Subcommittee on the Immigrant Community of African Descent." Vol. 4, Immigrants of African Descent. Albany, New York: New York Governor's Advisory Committee for Black Affairs, 1988. ERIC ED 348 412. Addresses the needs of black immigrants to New York State in four areas: (1) economic planning, (2) culture and the arts, (3) immigration reform, and (4) health care. Includes statistical data on New York State's black immigrant population.

875.   Stepick, Alex. "Haitian Boat People: A Study in the Conflicting Forces Shaping U.S. Immigration Policy." *Law and Contemporary Problems* 45, no. 2 (1982): 163-196. Reviews post-1972 United States efforts to return all Haitian boat people arriving in South Florida to Haiti, as economic rather than political refugees. Haitians' experiences, however, indicate their dual status as political and economic refugees. United States policy was supported by the ambiguity of relevant United States and international law as outlined in court decisions since 1963 that have denied Haitians refugee status. The 1977 administrative "Haitian Program," emphasizing expulsion from the United States, and court reaction to it further demonstrated this ambiguity. Additional ambiguity was reflected in the 1980 Cuban-Haitian entrant programs and the 1981 high-seas interdiction program.

876.   Stepick, Alex. "The New Haitian Exodus: The Flight from Terror and Poverty." *Caribbean Review* 11 (Winter) (1982): 14-17. The situation in Haiti since the revolution of 1804 has created ongoing migrations. The government has generally served the interests of the elite rather than the great population of subsistence peasants. After 1958, various sectors of society fled to the United States. The boat people are seen as both economic and political refugees because the society is categorized as a "kleptocracy" one "ruled by a government of thieves."

877.   Stepick, Alex, and Carol D. Stepick. "People in the Shadows: Survey Research among Haitians in Miami." *Human Organization* 49 (1990): 64-77. Describes the issues surrounding survey methodology in measuring the adaptation of Haitian migrants, with uncertain legal status, to Florida in the early 1980s. While Federal policies increased the problems of access and representativeness, Haitian culture and language led to unique problems of survey staffing, interpretation of questions and answers, and follow-up. Due to perceived discrimination, most Haitian primary social interactions were with other Haitians.

878.   Stepick, Alex. "The Refugees Nobody Wants: Haitians in Miami." Chap. 4 in *Miami Now! Immigration, Ethnicity, and Social Change*, edited by Guillermo J. Grenier and Alex Stepick III, 57-82. Gainesville, Fla.: University Press of Florida, 1992. Examines the relationships of contemporary Haitian immigrants in Miami Florida with the United States immigration authorities, the local native black population, various support groups, and the dominant society.

Most Haitians, including the middle class, experience perceptions of persecution and isolation but gain support from religious organizations and a small business class.

879.   Stepick, Alex. "Structural Determinants of the Haitian Refugee Movement: Different Interpretations." Occasional Papers Series, Dialogues #4. Miami, Fla.: Florida International University, Latin American and Caribbean Center, 1981. ERIC Research Paper, ED 263 278. Explains why Haitian boat people in south Florida were so uniquely persecuted and why government efforts to expel Haitians failed. The relative lack of economic opportunities in the Miami area produced tension at the local and national levels. Also examines the roles played by the courts, other advocates of Haitian rights, and related United States government legislation and policy.

880.   Stinner, William F., ed. "Return Migration and Remittances: Developing a Caribbean Perspective." RIIES Occasional Papers No. 3. Washington, DC: Smithsonian Institution, 1982. ERIC, ED 283 891. Includes thirteen papers discussing various issues related to Caribbean people who have migrated to the United States and then returned to live in their island nations. One of the papers discusses the flow of remittances to the Eastern Caribbean while another deals with remittances of Caribbean sugar cane cutters in Florida.

881.   Stone, Mike. "Still 'Goin' Foreign: An Examination of Caribbean Migration to North America." M.A. Thesis, Queen's University at Kingston (Canada), 1992. "An examination and analysis of the strong tradition of migration from the Caribbean...to North America" in the latter part of the 20th century. Examines the region's social structures that encouraged migration. Also examines "how return migration, remittances and development, or lack of it, enable and contribute to continuing mobility traditions."

882.   Sutton, Constance R. "The Caribbeanization of New York City and the Emergence of a Transnational Socio-Cultural System." Chap. 2 in *Caribbean Life in New York City: Sociocultural Dimensions*, edited by Constance R. Sutton and Elsa M. Chaney, 15-30. New York: Center for Migration Studies, 1987. The post-1965 influx of Caribbeans, and others, caused New York City to become a changed city of immigrants. Low-wage Caribbean labor encouraged new capital investment; the concentration of many nationality groups spawned a new Caribbean identity; and ongoing interaction with home societies led to a transnational immigrant culture as opposed to an assmilationist one. The city's racial/ethnic hierarchy led to an emphasis of ethnicity over race.

883.   Tobias, Peter M. "How You Gonna Keep Em Down in the Tropics Once They've Dreamed New York? Some Aspects of Grenadian Migration." Ph.D. Dissertation, Rice University (Houston, Texas): 1975. Finds Grenadian immigrants to New York City are not motivated by the classic "push-pull" hypothesis of migration, which emphasizes economic factors as the primary mo-

tivation for migration. Information on the potential migrant's destination is said to be created and transmitted during "liming" interactions in the rum shops of Montserrat, Grenada. Grenadians' New York experiences are said to be dominated by their view of this new environment as predatory.

884.   Villiers, Janice D. "Closed Borders, Closed Ports: The Plight of Haitians Seeking Political Asylum in the United States." *Brooklyn Law Review* 60, no. 3 (1994): 841-928. The United States continued to deny political refugee status to Haitian undocumented migrants in the early 1990s by relying on United States embassy officers' suggestions that human rights abuses were falsely reported. This study, arguing for a change in United States policy, examines relevant United States refugee and asylum law, the interdiction program of Haitians on the high seas, and uneven treatment of Haitian asylum seekers as influenced by class, language, and culture.

885.   Walsh, Bryan O. "Haitians in Miami." *Migration Today* 7, no. 4 (1979): 42-44. Describes the situation surrounding undocumented Haitians who fled to Miami, Florida by boat in the 1970s. Some fled directly from Haiti and others after being pressured to leave the Bahamas. The inconsistent treatment of these asylum seekers by United States Immigration officials is also discussed.

886.   Wiltshire, Rosina. "Implications of Transnational Migration for Nationalism: The Caribbean Example." *Annals of the New York Academy of Sciences* 645 (1992): 175-187. Explores Grenadian and Vincentian transnational migrant networks in New York City and Trinidad in terms of the benefits to women, childcare, and transnational traders. The family role as primary network link is reinforced by positive messages received by children in sending societies. The desire to enhance Caribbean identity and thus eschew racial underclass status led to numerous voluntary associations in New York City. New York migrants thus retained a Caribbean identity as opposed to dual nationalism expressed by migrants to Trinidad.

887.   Youseff, Nadia H. "Socio-Demographic Characteristics of New York's Foreign-Born Residents." Chap. 4 in *The Demographics of Immigration: A Socio-Demographic Profile of the Foreign-Born Population in New York State*, edited by Nadia H. Youseff, 75-94. New York: The Center for Migration Studies of New York, Inc., 1992. Presents comparative data on foreign-born New Yorkers with American-born New Yorkers and the nation's foreign-born by age composition, marital patterns, and educational attainments. Data from 1980 indicate a higher proportion of female foreign-born from Caribbean and Asian countries, with women dominating Caribbean immigration from the 1960s through the 1980s. The Caribbean foreign-born also significantly affected statistics on marital status and fertility. The higher educational level of English-speaking Caribbean immigrants is obscured when viewed regionally because of lower educational achievements of Hispanic Caribbeans.

888.   Zucker, Naomi F. "The Haitians versus the United States: The Courts as Last Resort." *Annals of the American Academy of Political and Social Science* 467(May) (1983): 151-162. Reviews United States policy and court cases, of the 1970s and early 1980s. Determines that the United States denied political asylum to most Haitian refugees because they were fleeing an ally, were poor and unskilled, and their admission would encourage other similar refugees. Despite court decisions favoring the Haitians' cause, the federal government continued illegal exclusionary practices.

Chapter 9

Politics

901.   Adler, Karen S. "Always Leading Our Men in Service and Sacrifice: Amy Jacques Garvey, Feminist Black Nationalist." *Gender & Society* 6, no. 3 (1992): 346-375. Declares that Marcus Garvey's second wife, also a Jamaican immigrant, was not just a helpmate but a key architect of Garveyism and a lifelong advocate of social justice. Also discussed is "the relationship between race, class, and gender as it pertains to Amy Jacques Garvey's life and social thought."

902.   Basch, Linda G. "The Politics of Caribbeanization: Vincentians and Grenadians in New York." In *Caribbean Life in New York City: Sociocultural Dimensions*, edited by Constance R. Sutton and Elsa M. Chaney, 160-181. New York: Center for Migration Studies of New York, 1987. Faced with a demeaning racial atmosphere, Vincentian and Grenadian New Yorkers find political participation in home societies more rewarding. Black Americans' low status in society and the dramatic increase in the number of West Indian immigrants lead to ambivalent intergroup relations. West Indian New Yorkers' political leadership role declined in the 1960s just as the their numbers increased dramatically. At that time, they began to respond to the new politics of ethnicity by emphasizing their uniqueness.

903.   Buhle, Paule. *C.L.R. James: The Artist as Revolutionary*. New York: Verso, 1988. An introduction to the life and creative output of this major radical political theorist from Trinidad who was an important political activist in the United States in the 1940s before moving on to Britain. Buhle also discusses James' literary and social criticism, fiction, biography, and polemical writing.

904.   Chisholm, Shirley. *The Good Fight*. New York: Harper & Row, 1973. The former Congresswoman continues the story told in her autobiography, with emphasis on her search for the Democratic Party's presidential nomination in 1972. This work concentrates on that losing nomination effort and describes

how disappointed and hurt the candidate was "at the coolness her candidacy received from both black male-led and white female-led organizations."

905.   Chisholm, Shirley. *Unbought and Unbossed.* Boston: Houghton Mifflin, 1970. The autobiographical account of the first black female member of the United States Congress, elected in 1968. This daughter of Barbadian immigrants served in the Congress for 14 years and was a staunch advocate for various progressive issues, including civil rights and women's liberation. The book also briefly examines the jobs of Congressperson, politician, and boss in the American political system.

906.   Clarke, John H. "Marcus Garvey: The Harlem Years." *Jamaica Journal* [Kingston] 8 (1974): 16-20. With Harlem as a base, the Jamaican Marcus Garvey's United Negro Improvement Association (UNIA) was the largest black mass movement in American history and significantly affected Harlem leaders and politics. Careers of several 19th century West Indian leaders in New York are described as antecedent to Garvey's. Garvey and the literary, artistic and political aspects of the Harlem Renaissance made Harlem world renown. An example was the UNIA's month-long international conference in 1920 that drew world attention to New York City.

907.   Cronin, Edmund D. *Black Moses: The Story of Marcus Garvey and the Universal Negro Improvement Association.* Madison: University of Wisconsin Press, 1955. A historical overview of the life and work of Jamaican Marcus Garvey, based upon the use of widely scattered materials. Concentrates on Garvey's various organizations and his trial for fraud but lacks a clear presentation of Garvey's philosophy and program.

908.   Cudjoe, Selwyn R., and William E. Cain, eds. *C.L.R. James: His Intellectual Legacies.* Amherst, Mass.: University of Massachusetts Press, 1995. A collection of critical essays on James' creative output in literature, criticism, cultural studies, political theory, history, and philosophy. Also contains the personal memoirs of his secretary, Anna Grimshaw.

909.   Davis, Lenwood G., and Janet L. Sims *Marcus Garvey: An Annotated Bibliography.* Westport, Conn.: Greenwood, 1980. A bibliographic chronicle of the Jamaican militant and founder of a major Pan-African movement, the United Negro Improvement Association (UNIA). Garvey migrated to New York City in 1916 where the UNIA became a defining political aspect of the Harlem Renaissance. This descriptive listing cites many speeches and articles by Garvey, including those that appeared in the New York City black press. The largest section describes 191 periodical articles about Garvey and his movement. Also included is the Constitution of the UNIA and a combined author/subject index.

910.   Dorsey, Francis E. "A Rhetoric of Values: An Afrocentric Analysis of Marcus Garvey's Convention Speeches, 1921-1924." Ph.D. Dissertation, Kent State University (Kent, Ohio), 1990. Using the concept of Afrocentrcity, this study attempts to eliminate racist ideas and language in its approach to understanding the significance of Marcus Garvey. An Afrocentric perspective is used to determine Garvey's persuasive appeal in the African community through his opening addresses at UNIA Conventions. Maintains that Garvey attempted to fulfill the four criteria of Afrocentricism in these addresses.

911.   Forsythe, Dennis. "West Indian Radicalism in America: An Assessment of Ideologies." In *Ethnicity in the Americas*, edited by Frances Henry, 301-332. The Hague: Mouton Publishers, 1976. Assesses the political radicalism of West Indian migrant activists who had significant presence in Harlem from the 1920s to the 1950s. Theorizes that both the migration process itself and America's change-inducing racism led to increasing West Indian militancy. The importance of culture, power and socialism all converged in the theories of W.A. Domingo, C.L.R James, Marcus Garvey, and Claude McKay, political activists in the 1920s' Harlem Renaissance.

912.   Garvey, Marcus. *The Philosophy and Opinions of Marcus Garvey or Africa for the Africans*. Reprint of 1923-1925 original ed. Dover, Mass.: Majority Press, 1986. Compiled by Garvey's second wife, Amy Jacques Garvey, who kept meticulous records of Garvey and the UNIA. Garvey was a black nationalist who espoused a variant of the success ethic that prevailed in white American society in the early 20th century, proposing positive paths for black economic success. Among other things, he also argued that the creation of a strong independent Africa would strengthen blacks everywhere. His political philosophy appealed to the black masses and less, if at all, to the black elite.

913.   Gladwell, Malcolm. "New York City Plays the New Ethnic Politics; As Wave of Immigrants Joins Electorate, Traditional Coalitions Have Less Meaning." *The Washington Post* (15 October 1993): 1. Sect.A, Col.3. Explores the impact on traditional ethnic politics in New York City that resulted from the large wave of immigration to the city during the 25 years prior to 1993. Includes a discussion of West Indians' self-perceived political and cultural distinctiveness from native-born blacks.

914.   Henry, Keith S. "The Black Political Tradition in New York: A Conjunction of Political Cultures." *Journal of Black Studies* 7 (1977): 455-484. Explores the influence of Caribbean blacks on the political life of black New Yorkers beginning in the 1930s. Among other things, Caribbean immigrants expanded black international perspective and added to the increasing professionalism of black political life in New York. The political and social transformation of black West Indian women is also explored.

915.   Henry, Keith S. "Caribbean Migrants in New York: The Passage from Political Quiescence to Radicalism." *Afro-Americans in New York Life and History* 2 (1978): 29-46. Explores the transition to political radicalism of English-speaking Caribbean immigrants to New York City from 1919 to 1940. Sees this transition as partly a response to newly acquired freedom of expression.

916.   Henry, Keith S. "Caribbean Political Dilemmas in North America and the United Kingdom." *Journal of Black Studies* 7 (1977): 373-386. Six articles explore the efforts of West Indian immigrants to adjust to North American politics and culture and to achieve ethnic consciousness. Political activism of English-speaking West Indians in New York and Quebec is assessed and compared with the activism of Haitian immigrants.

917.   Henry, Keith S. "The Place of the Culture of Migrant Commonwealth Afro-West Indians in the Political Life of Black New York in the Period Circa 1918 to Circa 1966." Ph.D. Dissertation, University of Toronto, 1973. (No abstract available. Potential readers should contact the their local public or college library to inquire if this title is available on interlibrary loan.)

918.   Hill, Robert A., et al., ed. *The Marcus Garvey and Universal Negro Improvement Association Papers*. Berkeley: University of California Press, 1983-. This projected 10-volume set will bring together over 30,000 documents dealing with the social, economic, and political forces that shaped and emerged from Garveyism. The first seven volumes constitute the American series, documenting the life and work of Garvey and the UNIA in the United States and then in Jamaica and England (1927-1940). Volumes 8 and 9 (published in 1995) and a forthcoming volume 10 document the role Africans played in Garveyism.

919.   Hill, Robert A., and Barbara Bair, eds. *Marcus Garvey: Life and Lessons; a Centennial Companion to the Marcus Garvey and Universal Negro Improvement Association Papers*. Berkeley: University of California Press, 1983. Two editors of the Garvey and UNIA papers collection present Jamaican-born Garvey's major essays from 1925 until his death in 1940. The writings include instructions for the African race, theories about the ideal state, a serialized autobiography, and others. Also included is a 95-page glossary of names and terms related to people and topics in Garvey's writings.

920.   Holder, Calvin. "The Rise of the West Indian Politician in New York City, 1900-1952." *Afro-Americans in New York Life and History* 4 (1980): 45-59. The migratory flow from the then British and Dutch West Indies to New York City between 1900 and 1952 is described. Focuses on immigrant participation in the black political life of New York and the immigrants' post 1930 rise to political power.

921.   Hooker, James R. *Black Revolutionary: George Padmore's Path from Communism to Pan-Africanism.* New York: Frederick A. Praeger, 1967. A personal and political biography of Trinidadian George Padmore, who lived in the United States in the 1920s. He studied at American universities and became a vigorous anticolonialist and Pan-Africanist. He organized pressure and protest groups and was an avid pamphleteer and journalist for the American black press. In 1928, he began editing the *Negro Champion,* later called the *Liberator,* in Harlem. Later he was a regular contributor of articles to *The Crisis.*

922.   Houpert, Karen. "Can She Fight the Power?" *Village Voice* 37 (1992): 13-14. Profiles the first Caribbean-born woman to serve on New York City's City Council as a symbol of immigrant success.

923.   Irish, J. A. George, and E. W. Bill Riviere, eds. *Political Behavior and Social Interaction among Caribbean and African American Residents in New York.* New York: Caribbean Research Center, Medgar Evers College, City University of New York, 1990. Three of the chapters in this preliminary study include: (1) The Rise and Fall of West Indian Politicians in New York (1900-1987); (2) Political Behavior Patterns of Caribbean Immigrants in New York in the Nineteen Eighties..., and (3) Socio-Political Relations Between African-American and African-Caribbeans in New York.

924.   James, C. Boyd. "Primitives on the Move: Some Historical Articulations of Garvey and Garveyism, 1887-1927." Ph.D. Dissertation, University of California, Los Angeles, 1982. This study sees Marcus Garvey's movement to be a struggle for equality based on the belief that the struggle was supported by natural laws of racial equity. Garveyism is thus seen as a natural way for black men and women to transform their reality as subjects of social oppression.

925.   James, C. L. R. *American Civilization* / edited and introduced by Anna Grimshaw and Keith Hart with an afterward by Robert A. Hill. Cambridge, Mass: Blackwell, 1993. C.L.R. James, the radical political activist and author, originally from Trinidad, wrote *American Civilization* in 1950 after his 1940s residence in the United States. His secretary (Anna Grimshaw) and Keith Hart edited it, following James' death. Broadly divided between political, literary, and cultural analysis, the book presents James' impressions of democracy in the United States.

926.   James, C. L. R. *The C.L.R. James Reader* / edited with and introduced by Anna Grimshaw. Cambridge, Mass.: Blackwell, 1992. A substantial anthology of James' works edited by his secretary, Anna Grimshaw. Includes numerous published and unpublished works such as James' letters to his second wife that expound his political dialectics. The collection includes an introductory essay that outlines James' political development.

927.   James, Christopher. "The West Indian Dilemma: Disunity." *Caribbean Today* 6, no. 10 (1995): 11-12. Discussed is the potential impact of a proposed ballot initiative in Florida that would deny certain tax-supported benefits to undocumented immigrants. The author maintains that while Hispanics have been united in their opposition to the proposal, West Indians have not.

928.   James, Winston. *Holding Aloft the Banner of Ethiopia: Caribbean Radicalism in Early Twentieth Century America*. New York: Verso, 1999. Outlines the economic and political forces that caused early 20th century Caribbean political radicals to migrate to the United States. Socio-political biography reveals the talents of people such as Hubert Harrison (the father of Harlem radicalism), Cryril Briggs and his African Blood Brotherhood, Marcus Garvey and the UNIA, and the radical intellectual/political activist C.L.R. James. Sharp distinctions are also drawn between Hispanic and British West Indian, and other non-Hispanic immigrants in this richly illustrated study.

929.   Kasinitz, Philip. "West Indian Diaspora: Race, Ethnicity and Politics in New York City." Ph.D. Dissertation, New York University, 1987. This study concludes that West Indian migrants to New York City before the great depression identified publicly and politically with the broader black community, while maintaining a clear sense of a distinct private identity. Those who migrated from the 1930's through the mid-1970s, however, formed a distinct ethnically-based public and political identity. Therefore the latter group was more differentiated from the indigenous black community and had a greater sense of West Indian national identity.

930.   Knight, Franklin W. "Introduction: The Caribbean Background of Richard B. Moore." In *Richard B. Moore, Caribbean Militant in Harlem: Collected Writings 1920-1972*, edited by W. Burghardt Turner and Joyce M. Turner, 2-15. Bloomington, Indiana: Indiana University Press, 1988. Explores the Barbadian background of Socialist American immigrant Richard B. Moore and the early history (1820s to 1920s) of Barbadian immigration to the United States. By the 1920s this immigration focussed on Harlem where Caribbean blacks developed a sense of West Indian identity and where Moore and others campaigned for independence for the English-speaking Caribbean and "liberation" for African Americans.

931.   Lewis, Rupert. "Claude McKay's Political Views." *Jamaica Journal* [Jamaica] 19 (1986): 39-45. An analysis of the antiracist, anticolonialist, and sometimes Communist views of Jamaican American Claude McKay, who was known primarily as a poet.

932.   Lewis, Rupert, and Maureen Warner-Lewis. "Amy Jacques Garvey." *Jamaica Journal* [Jamaica] 20 (1987): 39-43. Chronicles the life of Marcus Garvey's second wife who migrated to the United States from Jamaica in 1917, and soon became Marcus Garvey's private secretary and office chief of UNIA's

headquarters. She was Garvey's trusted confidant, edited a column in the *Negro World*, and advocated tirelessly for Pan-Africanism and Garvey. She was responsible for the preservation and publication of much of Garvey's work.

933.   Matis, Chris. "Awakening the Sleeping Giant: Deep in New York Neighborhoods a New Sense of Identity and the Growing West Indian Community is Emerging as a Political Force to be Reckoned With." *The Weekly Journal* (21 October 1993): 6-7. Notes that West Indians are recently seeking to "determine their own political future by registering to vote and running for political office in New York City and State." Points to the election of several West Indian candidates as evidence of this new agenda. Some of this political activism developed from a series of local racial incidents

934.   Matthews, Mark D. "Our Women and What They Think, Amy Jacques Garvey and the Negro World." *Black Scholar* 10 (1979): 2-13. Explores Amy Jacques Garvey's interpretation of the beliefs and motivations of female participant's in her husband's Universal Negro Improvement Association, during the 1920s. These interpretations were reflected in the "Women's Page" (edited by Amy Jacques Garvey) of the UNIA newspaper, *Negro World*.

935.   Mattson, Kevin. "The Struggle for an Urban Democratic Party: Harlem in the 1920s." *New York History* 76, no. 3 (July) (1995): 291-318. Chronicles the efforts of social/political leaders such as W.E.B. Du Bois and James Weldon Johnson (African Americans) as well as Hubert Harrison (West Indian) to develop a sense of civic pride that would allow Harlem to flourish. Their activism and oratory flourished in libraries, schools, and on street corners.

936.   Nutter, Jeanne Dolores. "Coverage of Marcus Garvey by the *New York "Age"* and *The New York "Times"*: A Comparative Historical Analysis." Ph.D. Dissertation, Washington, D.C.: Howard University, 1991. An analysis based on the theory that media "frames" or creates images of people and events by focusing on those aspects considered important. Concludes that the *New York Times* presented a more balanced picture of Garvey and his political/social/economic movement than did the *New York Age* (a black newspaper). Postulates that this difference reflected the conflicts between native-born blacks and West Indians and the different philosophies of Garvey and the indigenous black middle class.

937.   Ottley, Roi, and William J. Weatherby. "Post-War Era." In *The Negro in New York*, edited by Roi Ottley and William J. Weatherby, 209-228. Dobbs Ferry, N.Y.: Oceana Publications, 1967. Emphasizes the black political activism of Harlem, from 1918 to 1925, through a socio-political analysis of Marcus Garvey and other black West Indian radicals. Garvey's Universal Negro Improvement Association had special appeal to West Indian New Yorkers. Such Caribbean immigrants as W.A. Domingo and Claude McKay primarily edited the black radical press.

938.   Patterson, Orlando. "The Culture of Caution." *The New Republic* 213 (27 November 1995): 22-26. Views General Collin Powell's decision not to seek the United States Presidency in 1996, as probably being rooted in the Jamaican obsession with security. Explores the activities and traditions of West Indians in American politics during the early 20th century and again since the 1960's. Considers the demographic impact of this immigrant group and explains their evolution into transnational social systems.

939.   Perry, Jeffrey B. "Hubert Henry Harrison, 'The Father of Harlem Radicalism': The Early Years--1883 through the Founding of the Liberty League and *The Voice'* in 1917." Ph.D. Dissertation, Columbia University (New York City), 1986. A biographical study of this immigrant from St. Croix, Danish West Indies who many consider the father of Harlem political radicalism and the intellectual stimulus behind the New Negro Manhood Movement, of the early 20th century. Harrison strongly influenced early black leaders such as A. Philip Randolph and Marcus Garvey. Harrison was also the primary black organizer of the largest Socialist party local, Local New York.

940.   Phillips, Glenn O. "The Response of a West Indian Activist: D.A. Straker, 1842-1908." *The Journal of Negro History* 76, no. 2 (1981): 128-139. A profile of this Barbadian American political activist, attorney, educator, and journalist from about 1869 to 1908. As a graduate of Howard University School of Law, he served in the United States Department of the Treasury for four years. He was briefly a United States Congressman during Reconstruction from South Carolina and continued as an active advocate of black equality there and later in Detroit, Michigan. By mid-1884, he was considered the strongest and most articulate voice of black protest in the South. He served two terms as an elected circuit court commissioner (judge) in Wayne County, Michigan.

941.   Pierre-Pierre, Garry. "West Indians Adding Clout at Ballot Box." *The New York Times* (6 September 1993): 17. Sect.1, Col.4. Traditionally, West Indians have played a supporting political role in electing black candidates in New York City. However, by 1993, West Indians sought more directly to determine their own political outcomes by running for local office and registering to vote. They have, therefore, become a unique political force within local black politics. Explores the effect of this effort through the election of several politicians of West Indian decent since 1985. Includes a census tract map of New York City's five boroughs showing percentages of the West Indian population.

942.   Rhodes, Leara. "Role of Haitian Newspapers in the United States." *The Journalism Quarterly* 70, no. 1 (Spring) (1993): 172-180. The contents of four Haitian-American newspapers are analyzed to explore their roles in American communities and in Haiti. To summarize, these newspapers do not stress ethnic assimilation but function as alternative presses with political agendas.

943.   Samuels, Wilfred D. "Five Afro-Caribbean Voices in American Culture, 1917-1929: Hubert H. Harrison, Wilfred A. Domingo, Richard B. Moore, Cyril V. Briggs, and Claude McKay." Ph.D. Dissertation, The University of Iowa (Des Moines), 1977. Examines the dominant theses, programs, and pronouncements of these West Indian immigrants in early 20th century Harlem who actively participated in the "New Negro" movement. Chapter 3 discusses Hubert Harrison's "New Negro" program and Liberty League. Chapter 4 focuses on three of Harrison's radical political disciples: Cyril V. Briggs, Wilfrted A. Domingo, and Richard B. Moore. Chapter 5 briefly examines the political pronouncements of poet Claude McKay.

944.   Samuels, Wilfred D. "Hubert H. Harrison and the New Negro Manhood Movement." *Afro-Americans in New York Life and History* 5, no. 1 (1981): 29-41. Describes Harrison's work as a street corner orator and debater, political critic/activist, and scholar in efforts to improve the life of African Americans. He recruited blacks into the Socialist Party of America between 1912 and 1915, formed the Liberty League of Negro Americans in 1917, and worked as a journalist for the black press (1911-1927).

945.   Schiller, Nina G. "Ethnic Groups Are Made Not Born: The Haitian Immigrant and American Politics." Chap. 1 In *Ethnic Encounters: Identities and Contexts*, edited by George L. Hicks and Philip E. Leis, 23-35. North Scituate, Mass.: Duxbury Press, 1977. Examines how Haitian New Yorkers adapted to American politics by adopting an ethnic identity while being divided by class, education, color, and culture. Encouraged by the national Democratic Party, Haitians formed an ethnically based citizen's council in 1968 to gain access to the political system. A local politician's career demonstrates the benefits of organizing as an ethnic group in the face of African American disinterest.

946.   Seabrook, John H. "Black and White Unite: The Career of Frank R. Crosswaith." Ph.D. Dissertation, Rutgers The State University of New Jersey-New Brunswick, 1980. Various primary source material is used to profile the career of black labor leader, Frank R. Crosswaith. Born in the Virgin Islands, he immigrated to New York City in 1910, became a close ally of A. Philip Randolph, was a leading organizer in the Socialist Party, and a candidate for public office in New York City and State. He was the first black to hold a commissioner's post with the New York City Housing Authority.

947.   Stanley, Alessandra. "A Combustible Contest in a Smoldering Brooklyn." *The New York Times* (5 September 1991): 1. Sect.B, Col.2. Two Brooklyn neighborhoods, composed primarily of Caribbean immigrants, are reflected in the battle for a United States Congressional seat.

948.   Stein, Judith. *The World of Marcus Garvey: Race and Class in Modern Society*. Baton Rouge: Louisiana State University Press, 1986. Details the rise and fall of Marcus Garvey and his movement as an international black crusade. Includes portraits of key individuals who joined and/or abandoned Garvey along the way, yielding an understanding of the movement's social side. Garvey's movement is described in the context of his times but the theoretical structures of Garveyism and Pan-Africanism are missing.

949.   Toney, Joyce. "Similarities and Differences in the Response to Oppression among Blacks in the Diaspora." Chap. 16 in *Immigration and Ethnicity: American Society--"Melting Pot" or "Salad Bowl"*? edited by Michael D'Innocenzo and Josef P. Sirefman, 221-229. Westport, Conn.: Greenwood Press, 1992. Argues that the common experiences of West Indians and African Americans have outweighed their differences. Explores some of the aspects of slavery and emancipation that stimulated the growth of a black middle class in the West Indies and the urge to migrate. Despite some cultural and tactical differences, West Indians and native blacks have cooperated in political struggles from the 19th century into the 1970s.

950.   Turner, W. Burghardt, and Joyce M. Turner, eds. *Richard B. Moore, Caribbean Militant in Harlem: Collected Writings 1920-1972*. Bloomington: Indiana University Press, 1988. These collected works highlight the career of this prominent Harlem Communist who migrated from Barbados in 1909. They also explore Moore's Harlem business ventures and his reaction to American racism as the reason for his socialist activism. Discusses the effect of "soap box" orators on Moore and other West Indians, their forming of activist political organizations and "radical" publications and their relationships with the Jamaican activist, Marcus Garvey. Moore and his colleagues became orators, lecturers, and pamphleteers against racism and capitalist oppression.

951.   Vincent, Ted. "The Garveyite Parents of Malcolm X." *Black Scholar* 20 (1989): 10-13. An examination of copies of Marcus Garvey's *Negro World* (for 1926 and 1927) reveals that both parents of Malcolm X were active supporters of Marcus Garvey. Malcolm's father actively supported the Universal Negro Improvement Association (UNIA) in Omaha, Nebraska and Malcolm's mother worked as a reporter covering UNIA meetings and activities for the *Negro World*.

952.   Vincent, Ted. "Sandino's Aid from the Black American Press." *Black Scholar* 16 (1985): 36-42. Chronicles the role of Marcus Garvey's Harlem-based *Negro World* weekly as one of the most vocal supporters of Augusto Sandino's struggle against the invasion of Nicaragua by United States Marines (1927-1932). Among other things, the paper included speeches and letters Sandino had smuggled out of Nicaragua. Coverage of the struggle extended to the Women's Page, edited by Amy Jacques Garvey.

953.   Vincent, Theodore G. [Ted], ed. *Voices of a Black Nation: Political Journalism in the Harlem Renaissance.* San Francisco: Ramparts Press, 1973. A thematic grouping of excerpts from African American newspapers which thrived between 1917 and 1934 as the most potent communications medium for blacks. Many of the significant employees (editors and reporters) of these papers, were West Indians. An ongoing theme was the conflict between separatists and integrationists as exemplified in the Marcus Garvey-W.E.B. DuBois feud." An appendix lists black news agencies, magazines, and newspapers of the period, including the names of their editors."

954.   Von Drehle, David. "New York's Political Axiom: There Isn't Any; Successful Electioneering in the City Means Picking Up Fragments of Shattered Conventions." *The Washington Post* (5 April 1992): 16. Sect.A, Col.1. Political observers note that New York City's black vote has been historically split between Harlem and Brooklyn blacks. Harlem blacks were often descended from freed West Indians and produced some of New York City's first black office holders. Brooklyn blacks, historically descended from African American slaves, had often produced more radical political leaders.

955.   Walter, John C. "Black Immigrants and Political Radicalism in the Harlem Renaissance." *Western Journal of Black Studies* 1 (1977): 131-141. The Harlem Renaissance is seen as not only a cultural movement but also as one of political radicalism led primarily by West Indian immigrants. These post 1900 immigrants came from majority societies where they had not experienced the kind of racism they found in New York City. Their radical political activism, between 1900 and 1924 was expressed through new political parties, labor agitation and radical newspapers. Among the activists profiled is Ashley L. Totten who successfully pressured A. Philip Randolph to organize the Brotherhood of Sleeping Car Porters and Maids.

956.   Walter, John C. "Frank R. Crosswaith and the Negro Labor Committee in Harlem, 1925-1939." *Afro-Americans in New York Life and History* 3, no. 2 (July) (1979): 35-49. Chronicles the early career of this activist labor leader and proponent of Socialism, who emigrated from the Danish West Indies (The Virgin Islands). By 1925, he had founded the Trade Union Committee, which sought to unionize black workers and to choose a biracial union leadership. After working with A. Philip Randolph to build the Brotherhood of Sleeping Car Porters and Maids, he went on to organize the Harlem Labor Committee and then the Negro Labor Committee. The 1930s saw this latter committee struggling with bogus union leaders.

957.   Walter, John C. "Frank R. Crosswaith and Labor Unionization in Harlem, 1939-1945." *Afro-Americans in New York Life and History* 3, no. 2 (July) (1983): 47-58. By 1935 Crosswaith was a well-known social activist and the Negro Labor Committee had brought thousands of blacks into trade unions. The committee also promoted inter-racial worker solidarity and equality of black

and white trade union members. Crosswaith also played a national role in fighting racial discrimination in the defense industry of World War II. By 1945, he had meaningful impact on New York City politicians.

958.   Walter, John C., and Jill L. Ansheles. "The Role of the Caribbean Immigrant in the Harlem Renaissance." *Afro-Americans in New York Life and History* 1, no. 1 (1977): 49-66. Explores the leadership roles, played by West Indians, in two of the three phases of the Harlem Renaissance. The phases covered are (1) political movements and related protest literature, and (2) labor unrest. Among the individuals profiled are Hubert Harrison, Ashley Totten, Thomas Patterson, Frank Crosswaith, W.A. Domingo, Cyril Briggs, Claude McKay, Eric Walrond, and Arthur Schomburg.

959.   Worcester, Kent. *C.L.R. James: A Political Biography*. Albany: State University of New York Press, 1996. This study views James' dislike of formal politics as a component of his independent Marxism. He was also a historian and theoretician of Pan-African politics. This biography provides background on James' family life and his political projects and positions while living in the United States and Britain after leaving Trinidad in 1932.

Author Index

Note: Numbers refer to entries in the *Guide*, not to pages.

Adler, Karen S., 901
Alexander, Daryl A., 201
Allen, Ray, 241
Allman, James, 801
Anderson, Jervis, 802
Armand, Yolaine Pierre-Noel, 202
Arnold, Faye W, 501
Ashmeade, Roy W., 502

Bach, Robert L, 803
Baldwin, Anne, 401
Ballenger, Cynthia, 402
Baptiste, David A. Jr., 702
Barber, Beverly A., 242
Barnes, Grace M., 403
Barton, D., 228
Basch, Linda , 203, 902
Bashi, Vilna, 503
Berlin, Ira., 101
Berotte Joseph, Carole M., 404
Best, Tony, 504
Biafora, Frank A., 505
Bien-Aime, Joseph C., 405
Blauner, Peter, 302
Bogen, Elizabeth, 102, 204
Bonnett, Aubrey W., 303, 304,
    305, 306, 601

Borge, Michelle, 804
Boswell, Thomas D., 307, 805
Brana-Shute, Rosemary, 115
Brice-Baker, Janet, 703
Brimelow, Peter, 806
Brome, Henderson LeVere, 602
Brown, Karen McCarthy, 205
Brown, Patricia Leigh, 206
Broyles, William, 807
Bryce-Laporte, Roy S., 308, 506,
    808, 809, 810, 811
Buchanan, Susan H., 207, 243,
    507, 603, 812, 813
Buff, Rachel J., 257
Bumiller, Elisabeth, 258
Burgess, Judith, 375, 604
Burns, Allan F., 814
Butcher, Kristin F., 309
Buuhle, Paule, 903

Callahan, Walter, 406
Canton, Denise S., 704
Cardo, Lorelynn-Mirage, 509
Carlson, Alvar W., 244
Center for Afro-American and
    African Studies, 116
Chaney, Elsa M., 815

Charles, Carolle, 510, 511
Chavkin, Wendy, 705
Chi, Peter S. K., 706
Chierici, Rose-Marie Cassagnol, 512
Chisholm, Shirley, 904, 905
Chiswick, Barry R., 310
Ciesielski, S., 707
Clarke, John H., 906
Clarke, Velta, 208, 209
Colen, Shellee, 376, 377
Colwell, J. G. A., 229
Conway, Denis, 210, 817
Coombs, Orde, 211
Cooper, Wayne F., 245
Cordasco, Francesco, 117
Craige, Tito, 362
Cronin, Edmund D., 907
Cudjoe, Selwyn R., 908
Cummings, Alban, 407, 408

Dacosta-Bagot, Patricia A., 708
D'Amico, Thomas F., 311
Daneshvary, Nasser, 312
Dao, James, 259
Davis, Lenwood G., 909
DeFreitas, Gregory E., 313
Degazon, Cynthia Evonne, 513
Desantis, L., 605
Devine, John F., 409
DeWind, Josh, 363, 818
De Witt, Karen, 819
Divale, William, 709
Dodoo, F. Nil-Amoo, 314, 315,
  316, 317, 318
Domingo, W. A., 103
Dorsey, Francis E., 910
Dreyfuss, Joel, 820
Duany, Jorge, 821
Dubois, Laurent, 710
Dunn, Marvin, 319

Eaton, William W., 711
Eddie, David., 822
Edmonds, Arlene, 823
Edwards, Ione Dunkley, 410
Elwell, Patricia J., 824

Farmer, Paul, 712
Feen, Richard H., 825
Feigelman, William, 212
Fernandez-Kelly, M. Patricia, 826
Fjellman, Stephen M., 606
Folkes, Karl C., 411
Foner, Nancy, 320, 364, 378, 379,
  514, 515, 516, 517, 518, 607,
  827
Forsythe, Dennis, 321, 911
Foster, Charles R., 412
Foster, Joyce P., 413
Fouche, Marie, 414
Fouron, Georges Eugene , 608
Fradd, Sandra H., 415
Frankel, Bruce, 322
Frankenhoff, Charles A., 828
French, Howard W., 829
Fruchter, Rachel G., 713

Gans, Herbert J. , 323
Garcia, John A., 830
Garrot, Carl L., 416
Garvey, Marcus, 912
Gerlus, Jean-Claude, 324
Giles, Hollyce C., 417
Gladwell, Malcolm, 519, 913
Glantz, Oscar, 325, 520
Glick, Nina B., 521
Glick-Schiller, Nina, 246
Gonzalez, Nancie L., 522
Gopaul-McNicol, Sharon-Ann,
  523, 609, 714
Gordon, Antonio M. Jr., 715
Gordon, Monica H., 380, 418, 831
Grasmuck, Sherri, 326
Green, Charles, 716
Greene, Judy, 419
Griffith, David, 365, 366, 367, 368
Gumbert, Edgar B., 524
Gupta, Udayan, 327

Habenstreit, Barbara, 717, 718
Hahamovitch, Cindy, 369
Hall, Herman, 328
Hall, R. M. R., 420

Hamid, Ansley, 230, 231, 232
Hathaway, Heather A., 247
Hawkins, B. Denise, 421
Heim, Chris, 248
Hellman, Ronald G., 118
Helton, Arthur C., 833, 834
Henry, Keith S., 914, 915, 916, 917
Herlinger, Chris, 525
Herradas-Cruzalegui, Marco A., 329
Hill, Donald R., 260
Hill, Robert A., 918, 919
Hinds, Lester, 835
Hintzen, Percy, 526
Hiscox, Anna, 719
Ho, Christine G. T., 527, 610
Hoh, Harold Hongju, 836
Holder, Calvin B., 104, 528, 920
Honey, Ellen, 720
Hooker, James R., 921
Houpert, Karen, 922
Houston, Marion F., 837
Huggins, Winston G., 249
Hughes, Joyce A., 838

Irish, J. A. George, 923

Jackson, Joyce M., 214
James, C. Boyd, 924
James, C. L. R., 925, 926
James, Christopher, 927
James, Winston, 928
Jarecke, Walter H., 422
Jean-Baptiste, Carline, 529
Jenkins, Nancy H., 215
Johnson, Audrey, 381
Johnson, Creola, 721
Johnson, Violet Mary-Ann, 530
Jones, Alex S., 331
Jones, Charisse, 261
Jones-Hendrickson, S. B., 840
Jorge, Antonio, 841

Kail, Barbara L., 233
Kalmijn, Matthijs, 332

Kasinitz, Philip, 262, 333, 334, 531, 929
Kennedy, Randy, 263
Kessner, Thomas, 842
Kifner, John, 264, 532
Kim, Hugh K., 533
Kleiman, Dena, 335
Kleinman, Paula H., 722
Klockenbrink, Myra, 216
Klopner, Michele Anne Cuvilly, 843
Knight, Franklin W., 930
Kraly, Ellen P., 844

Lacovia, R. M., 611
Laguerre, Michel S., 105, 723, 845, 846, 847
Laidlaw, Walter, 119
Lang, Sandra, 724
Larmer, Brook, 612
Lassiter, Sybil M., 534
Lawless, Robert, 120, 848
Leavitt, Roy L., 535
LeSeur, Geta, 250
Leveque, Patricia Gill, 424
Levinson, David, 121
Lewis, Leonard C., 425
Lewis, Rupert, 931, 932
Light, Ivan H., 336
Little, Cheryl, 849
Lobo, Arthur Peter, 850
Loescher, Gilburt, 851
Lombardo, Shari, 426
London, Clement B. G., 427, 428, 536
Lord, Mavis Rosetta, 382
Lynch, Robert E., 429
Lyons, Beverly Pauline, 537

Mace-Matluck, Betty J., 430
Maingot, Anthony P., 852, 853, 854
Malcolm, Joan A., 613
Manning, Frank E., 265
Marshall, Adriana , 337
Marshall, Dawn I., 106

Marshall, Paule, 217, 383
Mason, Marco Antonio, 725
Matis, Chris, 933
Matthews, Lear, 726
Matthews, Mark D., 934
Mattingly, Vera Wilcher, 431
Mattson, Kevin, 935
Maynard, Edward Samuel, 614
McAlister, Elizabeth A., 538
McCallion, P., 615
McCoy, Terry L., 855
McGhee, Dorothy, 371
McKenzie, Victor M., 432, 433
McLaughlin, Megan Elaine, 434
McPherson-Blake, Patricia C., 616
Michael, Suzanne, 435
Michel, Claudine, 436
Miller, Jake C., 856
Millette, Robert E., 539
Millman, Joel, 857
Mirage, Lorelynn W., 540
Mitchell, Christopher, 858, 859
Mittelberg, David, 541
Model, Suzanne, 338, 339, 384
Mohl, Raymond A., 860
Mollenkopf, John H., 122
Morgan, Thomas, 218
Morrow, Robert D., 727
Mortimer, Delores M., , 861

Nagourney, Adam, 266
National Coalition for Haitian
   Rights, 123
Nelson, Emmanuel S., 251
Nero, Shondel J., 437
New York City Board of Educa-
   tion, 438
Nicholson, Marteen, 385
Nossiter, Adam, 862
Nutter, Jeanne Dolores, 936

Ojito, Mirta, 267
Olsen, Dale A., 439
O'Sullivan, Sean Patrick, 617
Oswald, L. R., 618
Ottley, Roi, , 107, 108, 937

Palmer, Ransford W., 340, 341,
   342, 863
Papademetriou, Demetrios G., 343, 864
Pareles, Jon, 268, 269
Patterson, Orlando, 938
Perry, Jeffrey B., 939
Petras, Elizabeth McLean, 386
Phillips, Glenn O., 940
Pierre-Pierre, Garry, 270, 619,
   620, 865, 941
Portes, Alejandro, 109, 344, 345,
   346, 441, 542, 728
Potocky, Miriam, 347
Powers, Thomas, 866
Pratt-Johnson, Yvonne, 442
Prou, Marc E., 443
Purdy, Matthew, 271

Quimby, Ernest, 234

Raphael, Lennox, 543
Regis, Humphrey A., 544, 545
Reid, Ira De A., 110
Reimers, David M., 111
Rhodes, Leara, 942
Ricketts, Erol, 867
Rieder, Jonathan, 546, 547
Robinson, Arnette D., 729
Rohlehr, Lloyd, 348
Roney, Lisa S., 868
Rorro, Gilda L., 444
Rosenthal, Beth S., 445
Roumain, Maryse-Noel, 730
Rounds, Connie C., 446
Ruducha, Jenny, 731
Rumbaut, Ruben G., 548

Salins, Peter D., 349
Salvo, Joseph J., 124, 869
Samuels, Wilfred D., 943, 944
Sandis, Eva, 220
Sansaricq, Rev Guy, 549
Schey, Peter A., 870
Schiller, Nina G., 550, 551, 621, 945
Scott, Clarissa S., 732
Seabrook, John H., 946

Seabrooks, Patricia Ann Johnson, 733
Seamonds, Jack, 236
Segal, Aaron, 125
Seligman, Linda, 447
Sengupta, Somini, 272
Shacknove, Andrew E., 871
Sims, Calvin, 552
Smikle, Patrick, 553
Smith, Abe, 237
Smith, Alanzo H., 622
Smith, J. Owens, 448
Smith, Michael P., 273
Sol, Ahiarah, 350
Sontag, Deborah, 351, 352, 449, 872, 873
Soto, Maria, 623
Sowell, Thomas, 353
Spurling, John Jasper, 554
Stafford, Susan B., 387, 555
Stange, Maren, 252
Stanley, Alessandra, 947
Stein, Judith, 948
Stepick, Alex, 354, 355, 356, 556, 875, 876, 877, 878, 879
Stevenson, Peggy L., 253
Stinner, William F., 880
Stone, Mike, 881
Sutton, Constance R., 557, 882

Tabor, Mary, 274
Tanton, J., 238
Taylor, Dorceta E., 558
Taylor, Dorothy L., 559
Thomas, Bert J., 221, 222
Thompson, Jonathan, 560
Thrasher, Shirley P., 624, 625, 734
Tobias, Peter M., 223, 883
Todd, Caron Thalia, 735
Toney, Joyce, 224, 949
Trabold, Robert, 225, 226, 254
Tucker, Barbara M., 373
Turner, W. Burghardt, 950
Twining, Mary, 255

Ueda, Reed, 112

University of California, Davis, 135
U.S. Dept. of Commerce, Bureau of the Census, 126, 127, 128, 129, 130, 131
U.S. Dept. of Justice, Immigration and Naturalization Service, 132, 133
U.S. Dept. of State, Bureau of Security and Consular Affairs, 134

Van Capelleveen, Remco, 275
Verdet, Paule. , 450
Vickerman, Milton D., 562, 563
Villiers, Janice D., 884
Vincent, Ted, 951, 952, 953
Von Drehle, David, 954

Waldinger, Roger, 357, 358, 359, 564
Walsh, Bryan O., 885
Walter, John C., 113, 955, 956, 957, 958
Warshaw, Bob, 239
Waters, Mary C., 565, 566
Watkins-Owens, Irma, 114
Watson, James, 374
Weatherby, Norman L., 736
Webb, John Badgley, 451
Welte, John W., 737, 738
Wenski, Thomas G., 227
White-Davis, Gerald Elroy, 452
Wilcken, Lois Eileen, 256
Wiltshire, Rosina, 886
Winer, Lise, 453
Witkin, Gordon, 240
Woldemikael, Tekle, 567, 568, 569
Worcester, Kent, 959

Yarrow, Andrew L., 276
Youseff, Nadia H., 360, 361, 570, 887

Zephir, Flore, 454, 571
Zucker, Naomi F., 888

Title Index

Note: Numbers refer to entries in the *Guide*, not to pages.

Accessing Mental Health and Development Disabilities Services: Some Haitian Issues and Concerns, 730

Adaptation of Jamaican Immigrants in American Schools: Problems and Possibilities, 452

Adjustment of Caribbean Immigrants in New York: Social & Economic Dimensions, 208

African American and West Indian Folklife in South Florida, 214

The African Caribbean Community (Philadelphia), 823

Agricultural Workers in World War II: The Reserve Army of Children, Black Americans, and Jamaicans, 373

AIDS and the Inner City: Critical Issues, 720

Alcohol Use Among Adolescent Minority Groups, 737

Alcohol Use Among Migrant Laborers in Western New York, 374

Alien Justice: The Exclusion of Haitian Refugees, 818

All In the Same Boat? Unity and Diversity in Haitian Organizing in New York, 550

Alway's Leading Our Men in Service and Sacrifice: Amy Jacques Garvey, Feminist Black Nationalist, 901

American Civilization (C.L.R. James), 925

American Immigrant Cultures: Builders of a Nation, 121

American Odyssey: Haitians in New York City, 845

The American Response to Haitian Refugee Migration, 871

Amnesty for Illegal Aliens from The Caribbean: Implications for Future Immigration Flows, 868

Amy Jacques Garvey, 932

An Analysis of Immigration: St. Kitts-Nevis to the U.S. Virgin Islands, 840

Ancestry of the Population in the United States, 126

Ann Sevi Ak Tout Entelijans Elev Ayisyen Yo: Yon Seri leson matematik ak syans pou elev edikasyon jeneral ak elev edikasyon espesyal (4em-8em ane) = Tapping into Haitian Students' Multiple Intelligences: A Collection of Mathematics and Science Lessons for General and Special Education Students (Grades 4-8)", 438

Anthropology, Accountability, and the Prevention of AIDS, 712

Anthropology and AIDS, 701

Apple Picker Blues, 371

The Art of West Indian Clients: Art Therapy as Nonverbal Modality, 719

Assimilation Differences Among Africans in America, 314

At 30, Caribbean Festival Is Bursting at Seams, 263

At Home with Edwidge Danticat: Haitian Tales, Flatbush Scenes, 620

An Atlas of International Migration, 125

Attitudes Toward the Elderly among Nursing Home Aides: A Factor Analytic Study, 729

Awakening the Sleeping Giant: Deep in New York Neighborhoods a New Sense of Identity ... to be Reckoned With, 933

The Barrel Children, 612

Becoming Black American: Haitians and American Institutions in Evanston, Illinois, 569

Beyond Nostalgia: The Old Neighborhood Revisited, 564

Beyond the Safety Valve: Resent Trends in Caribbean Migration, 821

A Bibliography of Caribbean Migration and Caribbean Immigrant Communities, 115

Black America and the Anglo-phone Afro-Caribbean Literary Consciousness, 251

Black Americans' Business Ownership Factors: A Theoretical Perspective, 350

Black and White Unite: The Career of Frank R. Crosswaith, 946

The Black Boat People Flounder on the Shoals of U.S. Policy, 870

Black Customers, Korean Grocers: Need and Mistrust; Shoppers Complain of Hostile Treatment, But Choices Are Few, 552

Black Immigrant Women in Brown Girl, Brownstones, 383

Black Immigrants and Political Radicalism in the Harlem Renaissance, 955

Black Immigrants and the American Ethos: Theories and Observations, 321

Black Immigrants in the U.S. Labor Market: An Earnings Analysis, 312

Black Immigrants in the United States: A Comparison with Native Blacks and Other Immigrants, 309

Black Immigrants: The Experience of Invisibility and Inequality, 506

Black Immigration and Ethnicity in the United States: An Annotated Bibliography, 116

Black Like Me: Race in America, 301

Black Like Them, 519

Black Miami in the Twentieth Century, 319

Black Moses: The Story of Marcus Garvey and the Universal Negro Improvement Association, 907

Black Papers: Business with a Mission, 331

The Black Political Tradition in New York: A Conjunction of Political Cultures, 914

Black Revolutionary: George Pad-more's Path from Communism to Pan-Africanism, 921

Blackboard Jungle Revisited: The Semiotics of Violence in an Urban High School, 409

Blacks against Korean Merchants: An Interpretation of Contributory Factors, 533

Blacks and Earnings in New York State, 315

Blood Relations: Caribbean Immigrants and the Harlem Community, 1900-1930, 114

Boat People Tough It Out: Haitian Immigrants Struggle to Survive in North Carolina, 362

Brooklyn Goes Caribbean on West Indian-American Day, 267

Calling Home: Migration, Race, and Popular Memory in Caribbean Brooklyn and Native-American Minneapolis, 1945-1992, 257

Campaign Launched to Raise Funds for Haitians, 508

Can She Fight the Power?, 922

The Cane Contract: West Indians in Florida, 363

Career Awareness through Research in Science and Math Achievement for Haitian High School Students in New York City (Project CARISMA): Final Evaluation Report, 426

The Caregiving Dilemma: Work in an American Nursing Home, 378

Carib Immigrants, African-Americans Still Divided, 553

Caribbean-American Associations: Activism or Parochialism?, 221

Caribbean Basin Refugees: The Impact on Health in South Florida, 715

Caribbean Development and the

Migration Imperative, 340

Caribbean Diasporas: Migration and Ethnic Communities, 109

Caribbean Exodus: U.S. Is Constant Magnet, 829

Caribbean Families Social and Emotional Problems, 714

The Caribbean Immigrant Impulse in American Life, 113

Caribbean Immigrants: A Black Success Story?, 384

Caribbean Immigrants in Higher Education: A Study of the Relationship among Their Learning Styles and Strategies, Achievement Motivation and Academic Performance, 425

Caribbean Immigrants in New York City: A Demographic Summary, 102

Caribbean Immigration to the United States, 808

Caribbean Migrants in New York: The Passage from Political Quiescence to Radicalism, 915

Caribbean Migration as Structural Reality, 852

Caribbean Migration: Causes and Consequences, 803

Caribbean Migration to the Mainland: A Review of Adaptive Experiences, 830

Caribbean New York, 531

A Caribbean Party; Crown Heights Parade Spreads Joy, 259

Caribbean Political Dilemmas in North America and the United Kingdom, 916

Caribbean Pupils' English Seems Barrier, Not Bridge, 449

Caribbean Verve Brightens New York, 218

The Caribbeanization of New York City and the Emergence of A Transnational Socio-Cultural System, 882

The Caribbeanization of New York
    City: West Indian Festival in
    Brooklyn, 275
Caribbeans in U.S. Prisons, 229
The Causes and Composition of
    West Indian Immigration to New
    York City, 1900-1952, 104
Cervix and Breast Cancer Inci-
    dence in Immigrant Caribbean
    Women, 713
Children of the Caribbean: A Study
    of Diversity, 407
Children of the New Wave Immi-
    gration: An Exploration, 435
A City of Immigrants Is pictured
    in Report, 872
City on the Edge: The Transforma-
    tion of Miami, 556
Claude McKay's Political Views, 931
Clinical Practice with Caribbean
    Immigrant Families in the United
    States: The Intersection of Emi-
    gration, Immigration, Culture,
    and Race, 702
Closed Borders, Closed Ports:
    The Plight of Haitians Seeking
    Political Asylum in the United
    States, 884
C.L.R. James: A Political Biogra-
    phy, 959
C.L.R. James: His Intellectual
    Legacies, 908
The C.L.R. James Reader, 926
C.L.R. James: The Artist as Revo-
    lutionary, 903
Cold Symptoms and Emotional
    Dissatisfaction among Rural
    Urban and Culturally Diverse
    High School Students, 709
A Combustible Contest in a Smol-
    dering Brooklyn, 947
Coming North: Latino & Carib-
    bean Immigration, 816
Communication and the Sense of
    Community among the Mem-
    bers of an Immigrant Group, 544

A Comparative Study of Health
    Care Behavior among Three
    Black Ethnic Groups, 717
A Composite Profile of Haitian Im-
    migrants in the United States
    Based on a Community Needs
    Assessment, 843
Conflicts of Culture, Class and
    Gender in Selected Caribbean
    -American and Caribbean
    Women's Literature, 253
Context and Opportunity:
    Minorities in London and New
    York, 338
The Context of Caribbean Migration,
    815
A Contrastive Haitian Creole-
    English Checklist, 420
The Contribution of Foreign-Born
    Workers to the Economy of New
    York, 360
Coping Strategies among Cultural-
    ly Diverse Inmates, 724
Counseling Haitian Students and
    Their Families: Issues and In-
    terventions, 417
Coverage of Marcus Garvey by
    the New York "Age" and The
    New York "Times": A Com-
    parative Historical Analysis,
    936
A Critical Investigation With a
    View to Address Tension Be-
    tween African-Americans
    and Caribbeans at the Brooklyn
    Temple Seventh-Day Adventist
    Church, 502
A Critical Study of Six Jamaican
    Artists in the Context of an
    Emerging Caribbean Culture in
    New York: An Aesthetic Inquiry,
    249
Cross-Cultural Differences in Effi-
    cacy Expectations of Achieve-
    ment Motivation Between
    Women, 382

Cross-Cultural Ministry in a Pluralistic Religious Community, 560

A Cross-Cultural Study of the Effects of Modeling, Reinforcement and Color Meaning Word Association on Doll Color Preferences of Black Preschool Children and White Preschool Children in New York and Trinidad, 523

Crosscurrents: West Indian Immigrants and Race, 562

Crown of Thorns: The Roots of the Black-Jewish Feud, 546

The Crucible within: Ethic Identity, Self-Esteem, and Segmented Assimilation among Children of Immigrants, 548

Crucibles of Caribbean Conditions: Factors of Understanding for Teaching and Learning with Caribbean Students in American Educational Settings, 427

Cuban, Haitian Refugees in Miami: Public Policy Needs for Growth from Welfare to Mainstream, 828

Cuisine of the Caribbean: It's Here and It's Hot; New York Embraces Island Fare, 215

Cultural Crossings: Migration, Generation, and Gender in Writings by Claude McKay and Paule Marshall, 247

The Cultural Meaning of Social Class for Haitians in New York City, 207

Cultural Mistrust and Racial Awareness among Ethnically Diverse Black Adolescent Boys, 505

Cultural Readjustment, Coping Strategies and Mental Health Status of West Indians Residing in a United States Metropolitan Area, 704

Culture Change, Ethnicity and Sociocultural Context: Acculturative Stress among Jamaican Immigrants, 708

Culture Clash; Tensions between Koreans and Blacks in U.S. Cities, 525

Culture, Health Care and the New Caribbean Immigrants: Implications for New Health Policy and Planning, 716

The Culture of Caution, 938

Culture Swapping: Consumption and the Ethnogenesis of Middle-Class Haitian Immigrants, 618

Cultures of Color, 534

Curriculum for Jamaican Creole-Speaking Students in New York City, 442

A Decade of West Indian Migration to the United States, 1962-1972: An Economic Analysis, 341

"Demele: Making It,"Migration and Adaptation among Haitian Boat People in the United States, 512

Dependents or Independent Workers?: The Status of Caribbean Immigrant Women in the United States, 380

Determinants of Leisure Participation: Explaining the Different Rates of Participation in African-Americans, Jamaicans, Italians and Other Whites in New Haven, 558

The Development of a Culture of Migration among a Caribbean People: St. Vincent and New York, 1838-1979, 224

The Development of a Framework for Health Care Advocacy on Behalf of Caribbean Immigrants, 725

Development of an Instrument Measuring Valence of Ethnicity and Perception of Discrimination, 509

Difference in Rates of Reported Disease among Regional Subgroups of the Black Population in Harlem, 735

The Differences in Social Service Utilization between Elderly United States Main Land Born Blacks and West Indian Born Blacks, 537

Different People: Studies in Ethnicity and Education, 524

Differential Adaptation of Grenadian Emigrant Communities in London and New York, 223

Disasporic Citizenship: Haitian Americans in Transnational America, 846

Divided Fates: Immigrant Children in a Restructured U.S. Economy, 826

Dr. Benjamin Watkins and the West Indian Community of New York City, 328

Drug Trafficking and the Caribbean Connection: Survival Mechanisms, Entrepreneurship and Social Symptoms, 234

Drug Trafficking in the United States, 239

Earnings Differences Among Blacks in America, 316

Echoes of Haitian Thunder, 107

Economic Characteristics of New York's Foreign-Born Residents, 361

The Economics of Market and Nonmarket Racial Discrimination, 311

The Editorial Dimensions of the Connection of Caribbean Immigrants to Their Referents, 545

Educational Progress of Children of Immigrants: The Roles of Class, Ethnicity, and Social Context, 441

Educator Asserts Immigrants Do Not Threaten Job Market, 335

Emigration to North America: The Continuing Option for the Caribbean, 817

Empowerment, Caribbean-Style: What African-Americans Can Learn from Black Immigrants, 526

Endogamy among Barbadian Immigrants to New York City: An Exploratory Study of Marriage Patterns and Their Relationship to Adjustment to an Alien Culture, 614.

English Language Development of Haitian Immigrant Students: Determining the Status of Selected Ninth Graders Participating in Transitional Bilingual Education, 443

Englishes in Contact: Anglophone Caribbean College Students in Metropolitan New York, 437

Establishing New Lives: Selected Readings on Caribbean Immigrants in New York City, 209

Ethnic and Racial Identities of Second-Generation Black Immigrants in New York City, 565

An Ethnic "Boiling Pot": Cubans and Haitians in Miami, 860

Ethnic Differences in Factors Related to Drug Use, 722

Ethnic Gangs and Organized Crime, 236

Ethnic Geography, 204

Ethnic Groups Are Made Not Born: The Haitian Immigrant and American Politics, 945

Ethnic Identification, Ethnicity, and Ethnic Solidarity in Los Angeles County's West Indian-American Community, 501

Ethnic Transformations in Late-Twentieth-Century Florida, 814

Ethnic, Racial Attitudes among Professional and Managerial Black Women: Research Note, 381

Ethnocultural Factors in Counseling With Male West Indian American Adolescents, 432

Ethnographic Findings on West Indian-American Clients, 433

Ethnographic Interviews with West Indian Families and a Workshop for Practitioners, 624

Everywhere We Go, We Are in Danger": Ti Manno and the Emergence of a Haitian Transnational Identity, 246

An Examination of Rotating Credit Associations among Black West Indian Immigrants in Brooklyn, 303

Exile, Ethnic, Refugee: The Changing Organizational Identities of Haitian Immigrants, 551

Expectations of Haitian Parents in the Greater New York Metropolitan Area: Education and Occupations, 451

An Exploratory Study of Teacher Accommodation to the Cultural and Linguistic Differences of Jamaican Children Using a Clinical Supervision/Group Discussion Strategy, 410

Exploring the Impact of Culture and Acculturation on Older Families Caregiving for Persons with Developmental Disabilities, 615

Fear, Crime, Community Organization, and Limitations on Daily Routines, 233

Female Immigrants to the United States: Caribbean, Latin America, and African Experience, 861

Female Predominance in Immigration to the United States Since 1930: A First Look, 837

A Festive Caribbean Immigrant Community in New York City: A Self Image, 254

Five Afro-Caribbean Voices in American Culture, 1917-1929: Hubert H. Harrison, Wilfred A. Domingo, Richard B. Moore, Cyril V. Briggs, and Claude McKay, 943

Flight into Despair: A Profile of Recent Haitian Refugees in South Florida, 354

The Flower in the Boat: Folk Art of the Migrant Workers of Mid-New York State, 255

For Thanksgiving, Two Feasts Two Traditions; A Spicy Blend of Caribbean and Black-American Flavors, 201

For West Indians, Cricket Field is Bit of Home, 213

The Foreign-Born Population (Internet Site), 127

Foreign Student Profile, 401

The Formation of Haitian Ethnic Group, 521

Frank R. Crosswaith and Labor Unionization in Harlem, 1939-1945, 957

Frank R. Crosswaith and the Negro Labor Committee in Harlem, 1925-1939, 956

From Ellis Island to LAX: Immigrant Prospects in the American City, 357

From Ganja to Crack: Caribbean Participation in the Underground Economy in Brooklyn, 1976-1986. Part 1. Establishment of the Marijuana Economy, 230

From Ganja to Crack: Caribbean Participation in the Underground Economy in Brooklyn, 1976-1986. Part 2. Establishment of the Cocaine (and Crack) Economy, 231

From Ghetto Elite to Service Sector: A Comparison of the Role of Two Waves of West Indian Immigrants in New York City, 333

From Other Shores, 327

From Policy Frontier to Policy Dilemmas: The United States and Caribbean Migration, 1960-1990, 858

Garifuna Settlement in New York: A New Frontier, 522

The Garveyite Parents of Malcolm X, 951

A Geographical Analysis of America's Ethnic Radio Programming, 244

Geopolitics, Economic Niches, and Gendered Social Capital among Recent Caribbean Immigrants in New York, 326

Ghetto Blasters, 857

The Good Fight (Shirley Chishiolm), 904

Haiti: A Research Handbook, 120

Haitian Americans, 723

Haitian and Dominican Undocumented Aliens ,in New York City: A Preliminary Report, 824

The Haitian Apostolate in Brooklyn, 549

Haitian Boat People: A Study in the Conflicting Forces Shaping U.S. Immigration Policy, 875

Haitian Creole Language and Bilingual Education in the United States: Problem, Right, or Resource?, 454

The Haitian Crisis: A Catholic Response, 832

Haitian Educators Work for Education Reform in Time of Crisis, 421

Haitian Ethnic Identity, Usage of Haitian Creole, Family Cultural Values, Level of self-Esteem, and Locus-of-Control in Haitian College Students, 529

Haitian Family Patterns of Migration to South Florida, 606

Haitian Immigrant Women: A Cultural Perspective, 387

Haitian Immigrants in Black America: A Sociological and Sociolinguistic Portrait, 571

The Haitian Informal Sector in Miami. City & Society, 355

Haitian Migrants and Haitian-Americans: From Invisibility into the Spotlight, 848

Haitian Migrants Settle in, Looking Back, 351

Haitian Migration: 30 Years Assessed, 801

The Haitian Niche in New York City, 847

The Haitian Refugee Litigation: A Case Study in Transnational Public Law Litigation, 836

Haitian Refugees Find Welcome Wears Thin, 619

Haitian Refugees: (Haiti's) Missing Persons, 804

Haitian Women in New York City, 603

Haitians, 105

Haitians: A Neglected Minority, 447

Haitians in Miami, 885

Haitians in New York City, 535

Haitians in the Arts, 243.

Haitians: Seeking Refuge in the United States, 838

The Haitians: The Cultural Meaning of Race and Ethnicity, 555

The Haitians versus the United States: The Courts as Last Resort, 888

A Handbook for Teachers of Haitian Students in New Jersey, 444

Heading to Florida, Nearer the Homeland, 865

Health and Healing Practices among Five Ethnic Groups in Miami, Florida, 732

Health Care and Health Status of Migrant Farmworkers in New York State, 706

Health Care Patterns of Non-Urgent Patients in an Inner City Emergency Room, 718

Historical Functions of Caribbean-American Benevolent/Progressive Associations, 222

Historical Statistics on the Foreign-Born Population of the United States: 1850 to 1990, 128

The History of Caribbean Migrations: The Case of the West Indies, 106

Holding Aloft the Banner of Ethiopia; Caribbean Radicalism in Early Twentieth Century America, 928

Housekeeping for the Green Card: West Indian Household Workers, the State, and Stratified Reproduction in New York, 376

How You Gonna Keep Em Down in the Tropics Once They've Dreamed New York? Some Aspects of Grenadian Migration, 883

Hubert H. Harrison and The New Negro Manhood Movement, 944

Hubert Henry Harrison, 'The Father of Harlem Radicalism': The Early Years--1883 through the Founding of the Liberty League and 'The Voice' in 1917, 939

Human Rights, U.S. Foreign Policy, And Haitian Refugees, 851

'I Never Knew They Existed': The Invisible Haitian Migrant Worker, 370

I Was Afraid but More I Was Hungry: Brooklyn's West Indians, 842

Identifying the Vocational Potential of a Disadvantaged Population, 422

If You're Thinking of Living in: Crown Heights, 216

Illegal Migration from the Caribbean, 863

The Immigrant Family: Cultural Legacies and Cultural Change, 607

Immigrants in the U.S. Labor Market, 310

Immigrants and Refugees: The Caribbean and South Florida, 839

Immigrants Look Outside New York for Better Life, 819

Immigration and Criminality in the U.S.A., 238

Immigration and HIV among Migrant Workers in Rural Southern Florida, 736

Immigration and Naturalization Statistics, 132

Immigration Fact Sheet, 133

Immigration from the Caribbean Basin, 853

The Immigration of Caribbean People to the U.S.: Some Comments, 809

Immigration, Refugee and Generation Status as Related to Behavioral Disorders, 727

Immigration to New York City in the '90s: the Saga Continues, 850

Immigration to New York City in the Post-1965 Era: Sex Selectivity and the Economic Role of Women, 869

Implementing the Professional Standards for Teaching Mathematics: Teaching Middle School Students with Diverse Cultural Backgrounds, 406

Implications of Transnational Migration for Nationalism: The Caribbean Example, 886

In Brooklyn, Harkening to the Steel-Drum Beat, 276

In Brooklyn, Steel Drums and a Truce, 264

In Living Colors: New York's Surprising Ethnic Future; New York City, 349

In Search of the Means to a Better Life: Caribbean Migration to the United States, 831

In the Eye of the Storm: The Context of Haitian Migration to Miami, Florida, 307

In the Valley of the Giant: The Politics of Migrant Farm Labor, 1865-1945, 369

The Influence of Social Support on School Completion among Haitians, 445

Institutional Adaptation of West Indian Immigrants to America: An analysis of Rotating Credit Associations, 304

Instructing Our Newest Minority: The Haitian, 446

Instruction of Haitian Bilingual Children in the United States, 412

Intelligibility of Reggae Lyrics in North America: Dread Ina Babylon, 453

International Labor Migration and Rural Development: Patterns of Expenditure Among Jamaicans Working Seasonally in the United States, 365

The Internationalization of Kinship and the Feminization of Caribbean Migrants: The Case of Afro-Trinidadian Immigrants in Los Angeles, 610

The Intersection of Gender, Race, and Ethnicity in Identity Development of Caribbean American Teens, 566

Introduction: New Immigrants and Changing Patterns in New York City, 514

Introduction: The Caribbean Background of Richard B. Moore, 930

An Introduction to Latin American and Caribbean Musics in Florida: Multicultural Approaches in the Music Classroom, 439

The Invisible Immigrants, 820

Island Sounds in the Global City: Caribbean Music and Identity in New York, 241

Islands in the City (Brooklyn West Indians), 302

Issues of Assessment and Identification of Anglo-Caribbean Students in a Migratory Educational Environment, 411

It's Carnival Time as New York Turns Caribbean to Dance the Weekend Away, 268

Jamaican and Black-American Migrant Farm Workers: A Comparative Analysis, 364

Jamaican Emigres Bring Thrift Clubs to New York, 330

A Jamaican Way Station in the Bronx: Community of Striving Immigrants Fosters Middle-Class Values, 862

Jamaican Women in the U.S. Health Industry: Caring, Cooking and Cleaning, 386

Jamaican Youth flee U.S. Sex and Drugs Trap: Teenage Immigrants are Being Sent Home to Escape the Dark Side of the American Dream, 237

Jamaicans in New York City, 827

Jamaicans in South Florida, Take a Bow!, 348

The Jamaicans: Race and Ethnicity among Migrants in New York City, 515

"Just a Little Respect": West Indian Domestic Workers in New York City, 377

Kansas City Experience: 'Crack' Organized Crime Cooperative Task Force, 228

Language and Identity: Haitians in New York City, 507
Learning About Haitians in New York State, 423
The Lilting Sound and Soul of Immigration, 274
Locus of Control and Aspiration to Traditionally Open and Traditionally Closed Occupations, 325

Maintenance and Change of Status in a Migrant Community: Haitians in Evanston, Illinois, 568
Mama Lola: A Voudou Priestess in Brooklyn, 205
Marcus Garvey: An Annotated Bibliography, 909
The Marcus Garvey and Universal Negro Improvement Association Papers, 918
Marcus Garvey: Life and Lessons; a Centennial Companion to the Marcus Garvey and Universal Negro Improvement Association Papers, 919
Marcus Garvey: The Harlem Years, 906
Maternal Separation and Bonding, Perceived Social Support, Anxiety and Depression in Caribbean Immigrant College Students, 613
The Men Who Created Crack, 240
Mental Health in Mariel Cubans and Haitian Boat People, 711
Mental Illness and Help-seeking Behavior Among Mariel Cuban and Haitian Refugees in South Florida, 728

Miami's Two Informal Sectors, 356
Migrant Child Health: The Role of Social, Cultural, and Economic Factors, 731
Migrant Farmworkers in the Oak Orchard Health Service Area. A Descriptive Profile and Assessment of Health Care Needs and Economic Impact, 372
The Migrant Heritage Studies Kit: A Teaching Tool, 429
Migration and Sex Roles: A Comparison of Black and Indian Trinidadians in New York City, 604
Migration and Transmutation in the Novels of McKay, Marshall and Clarke, 611
Migration and West Indian Racial and Ethnic Consciousness, 557
The Migration Experience: Social and Economic Adjustment of British West Indian Immigrants in Boston, 1915-1950, 530
Migration News, 135
Migration of Caribbean Women in the Health Care Field: A Case Study of Jamaican Nurses, 385
Minority Immigrants in the United States: Earnings Attributes and Economic Success, 317
The Minority Within: The New Black Immigrants, 334
Music Folklore among Haitians in New York: Staged Representations and the Negotiation of Identity, 256
My First Journey: A Haitian Immigration Story. A Learner-Centered Model Guide for Teachers, 414

National Coalition for Haitian Rights (Internet Site), 123
Nationality, Ethnicity and Race in the Demography of Immigration, 570

Native Sons and Immigrants: Some Beliefs and Values of American-Born and West Indian Blacks at Brooklyn College, 520

The Negro Immigrant: His Background, Characteristics and Social Adjustment, 1899-1937, 110

Neighborhood Immigrant Popular Religion: A New Interpretation, 225

The Never Ending Story: The Haitian Boat People, 825

The New American Immigration Evolving Patterns of Legal and Illegal Emigration: A Bibliography of Selected References, 117

New Cabbies Reflect Change in the Mosaic of New York, 352

New Faces, 108.

The New Female West Indian Immigrant: Dilemmas of Coping in the Host Society, 601

The New Haitian Diaspora: Florida's Most Recent Residents, 805

The New Haitian Exodus: The Flight from Terror and Poverty, 876

New Immigrants in New York's Economy, 337

The New Immigrants: Tensions and Opportunities for the Church in America, 227

New Immigrants to Brooklyn and Queens: Policy Implications, Especially with Regard to Housing, 864

New Orleans' Carnival Culture from the Underside, 273

The New Second Generation: Segmented Assimilation and Its Variants, 346

New York City and the New Caribbean Immigration: A Contextual Statement, 308

New York City in the 1980s: A Social, Economic, and Political Atlas, 122.

New York City Plays the New Ethnic Politics; As Wave of Immigrants Joins Electorate, Traditional Coalitions Have Less Meaning, 913

New York Haitians Proud: We Try Hard, 322

New York's Carnival, All Grown Up, 269

New York's Political Axiom: There Isn't Any; Successful Electioneering in the City Means Picking Up Fragments of Shattered Conventions, 954

The Newest New Yorkers: An Analysis of Immigration into New York City During the 1980s, 124

Of Worlds Seen and Unseen: The Educational Character of Haitian Vodou, 436

On Afro-American and Afro-Caribbean Cooperation, 536

One Mother, Two Daughters: The Afro-American and The Afro-Caribbean Female Bildungsroman, 250

Opportunity versus Constraint: Haitian Immigrants and Racial Ascription, 569

The 'Other Side' of Embeddedness: A Case Study of the Interplay of Economy and Ethnicity, 358

Our Women and What They Think, Amy Jacques Garvey and the Negro World, 934

Overseas Caribbean Carnivals: The Art and Politics of a Transnational Celebration, 265

Parade Is Stumping Ground for Mayoral Candidates, 266

Parade Shows Off West Indian Political Clout, 271

Pastoral Strategies in the Immigrant Work, 226

Patterns and Predictors of Alcohol Use Among 7-12th Grade Students in New York State, 403

Patterns of Adaptation of Haitian Immigrants of the 1970s in New York City, 608

Pearl Primus, In Search of Her Roots: 1943-1970, 242

Peasants in Reserve: Temporary West Indian Labor in the U.S. Farm Labor Market, 366

People in the Shadows: Survey Research among Haitians in Miami, 877

Perceptions of Latin American Business Graduates as Related to Adequacy of Employment in the New York City Metropolitan Area during the Years 1965-1971, 329

The Performance of English-Speaking Caribbean-American Students in the Psychoeducational Process, 424

The Persistence of Status in Social Stratification: A Case Study of Haitian Society, 202

Personal-Social Adjustment and Educational Achievement of West Indian Children in Selected Parochial Schools in New York City, 408

Perspectives on Recent Refugees and Immigrant Waves into South Florida, 841

The Philosophy and Opinions of Marcus Garvey or Africa for the Africans, 912

Phonemics within the Transitional Bilingual Program: From Haitian Creole to English, 416

Pilgrims from the Sun: West Indian Migration to America, 342

The Place of the Culture of Migrant Commonwealth Afro-West Indians in the Political Life of Black New York in the Period Circa 1918 to Circa 1966, 917

The Plight of Haitian Refugees, 856

Political Behavior and Social Interaction among Caribbean and African American Residents in New York, 923

The Political Economy of Crack-Related Violence, 232

The Political Economy of Haitian Migration: A Cross-Frontier Study of the Circulation of People, Capital, and Commodity Flows, 324

The politics of Caribbeanization: Vincentians and Grenadians in New York, 902

The Politics of Income and Education Differences between Blacks and West Indians, 448

Population of the City of New York, 1890-1930, 119

Post-War Era, 937

Potential for Intergenerational Conflict in Cuban and Haitian Immigrant Families, 605

Primitives on the Move: Some Historical Articulations of Garvey and Garveyism, 1887-1927, 924

The Process of Ethnogenesis Among Haitian and Israeli Immigrants in the United States, 541

Profile: Antoine Adrien, 219

Profile of a Haitian Migrant Woman, 812

Project Avaanse. Final Evaluation Report, 1993-94. OER Report, 419

The Promise of a Country: The Impact of Seasonal U.S. Migration on the Jamaican Peasantry, 367

Promise Of America, 807

Psychodynamic Therapy and Culture in the Treatment of Incest of a West Indian Immigrant, 734

PsychoSocial Factors Associated With the Immigration of Haitians and Jamaicans to South Florida and Changes in Their Parental Roles, 616

The Puerto Rican Parade and West Indian Carnival: Public Celebrations in New York City, 262

Quarantining HIV-Infected Haitians: United States' Violations of International Law at Guantanamo Bay, 721

Race and Color: Jamaican Migrants in London and New York City, 516

Race and Ethnic Relations in Immigrant New York, 517

Race and Immigrant Stratification in the United States, 318

Racial Mistrust and Disposition to Deviance Among African American, Haitian, and Other Caribbean Island Adolescent Boys, 559

Rap 'n' Reggae: Shinehead Pushes the Boundaries of Streetwise Music from the South Bronx All the Way to His Native Jamaica, 248

Rasta Crime: A Confidential Report by the N.Y.C. P.D., 235

Recent Third World Immigration to New York City, 1945-1986: An Overview, 111

Refugee Children: How Are They Faring Economically as Adults? 347

Refugees from Unrest: Central American & Caribbean Immigrants in the U.S., 822

The Refugees Nobody Wants: Haitians in Miami, 878

The Relationship of Ethnicity, Social Support, and Coping Strategies among Three Subgroups of Black Elderly, 513

Report of the Visa Office, 134

A Reporter at Large: The Haitians of New York, 802

Reproductive Health: Caribbean Women in New York City, 1980-1984, 705

The Response of a West Indian Activist: D.A. Straker, 1842-1908, 940

The Responses of West Indian Men Towards African-Americans: Distancing and Identification, 563

Return Migration and Remittances: Developing a Caribbean Perspective, 880

A Rhetoric of Values: An Afrocentric Analysis of Marcus Garvey's Convention Speeches, 1921-1924, 910

Richard B. Moore, Caribbean Militant in Harlem: Collected Writings 1920-1972, 950

The Rise of the West Indian Politician in New York City, 1900-1952, 920

Rising Islanders of Bed-Stuy, 217

Role of Haitian Newspapers in the United States, 942

The Role of the Academy in the Construction of Ethnicity among Black Caribbean Immigrants in the Urban United States: An Ethnographic Account of Commonwealth State College, 413

The Role of the Caribbean Immigrant in the Harlem Renaissance, 958

Rotating Credit Associations, 336

Salt-Water Trinnies: Afro-Trinidadian Immigrant Networks and Non-Assimilation in Los Angeles, 527
Sandino's Aid from the Black American Press, 952
The Scandal of U.S. Immigration: The Haitian Example, 866
Scattered Seeds: The Meaning of the Migration for Haitians in New York City, 813
School University Partnerships to Promote Science with Students Learning English, 415
Second-Generation Decline: Scenarios for the Economic and Ethnic Futures of the Post-1965 American Immigrants, 323
Selected Characteristics for Persons of British West Indian Ancestry: 1990, 130
Selected Characteristics for Persons of Dutch West Indian Ancestry: 1990, 131
Self-Esteem, Academic Adjustment, and Acculturation Among Haitian Students at Kingsborough Community College CUNY, 431
The Seroprevalence of Cysticercosis, Malaria, and Trypanosoma-Cruzi among North Carolina Migrant Farmworkers, 707
Sex Roles and Sensibilities: Jamaican Women in New York and London, 379
Shadow and Substance, 252
Should Immigrants Assimilate?, 542
Similarities and Differences in the Response to Oppression among Blacks in the Diaspora, 949
The Social Characteristics of Black Catholics, 212
Social Identities, Moral Narratives,

Scientific Argumentation: Science Talk in a Bilingual Classroom, 402
Social Organizational Obstacles to Capital Accumulation among returning Migrants: The British West Indies Temporary Alien Labor Program, 368
Social Relationships between American Negroes and West Indian Negroes in a Long Island Community: An Exploratory Examination of IntraGroup Relationships in the Addisleigh Park Neighborhood of St. Albans, Long Island, New York, 554
Social Stratification among First Generation Grenadians in Brooklyn: A Look at Adaptation to Deal with the New Society, 539
Social Supports of Older Haitians in Port-au-Prince and Miami: Effects on Health Practices and Perceived Health Status, 733
Social Workers' Knowledge of Client Culture and Its Use in Mental Health Care of English-Speaking Caribbean Immigrants, 726
Socio-Demographic Characteristics of New York's Foreign-Born Residents, 887
A Sociocultural Analysis of Family and Friendship Influences on Teenage Deviance, 617
The Socioeconomic Assimilation of Caribbean American Blacks, 332
Some Sociological Observations on Voluntary Organizations Among Recent Immigrants in New York, 220
A Spoonful of Blood: Haitians, Racism and AIDS. Science as Culture, 710
Statistical Abstract of the United States, 129

Status Needs Positive Change. Report of the Subcommittee on the Immigrant Community of African Descent, 874

Still "Goin' Foreign": An Examination of Caribbean Migration to North America, 881

Still the Promised City? African-Americans and New Immigrants in Postindustrial New York, 359

Stranger and Pilgrim: The Life of Claude McKay, 1890-1948, 245

Strategies to Improve the Self-Esteem of Ninth and Tenth Grade Haitian Limited English Proficient Students Through a Self-Concept Program, 405

The Stress Factor in Migration: A Dissenting View, 854

Structural Determinants of the Haitian Refugee Movement: Different Interpretaions, 879

The Structure of the Free Negro Caste in the Antebellum United States, 101

Structured Adaptation of Black Migrants from the Caribbean: An Examination of an Indigenous Banking System in Brooklyn, 305

The Struggle for an Urban Democratic Party: Harlem in the 1920s, 935

A Study of the Assimilation of Barbadian Immigrants in the United States with Special Reference to the Barbadians in New York, 602

Study Sees Illegal Aliens in New Light, 873

Success of West Indian Parade Brings Dissension, 270

A Survey of Self-Reports of Language Use, Self-Reports of English, Haitian, and French Language Proficiencies and Self-Reports of Language Attitudes Among Haitians in New York, 404

Teaching and Learning with Caribbean Students, 428

Tension in Brooklyn; Blacks March by Hasidim through a Corridor of Blue, 532

Terrains of Blood and Nation: Haitian Transnational Social Fields, 621

A Theory of Immigration and Racial Stratification, 503

Three Brooklyn Museums to Explore Crown Hts. Roots, and Nerves, 561

Three Years Later: The Adaptation Process of 1980 (Mariel) Cuban and Haitian Refugees in South Florida, 344

Through the Golden Door: Educational Approaches for Immigrant Adolescents with Limited Schooling, 430

Time to Rethink Immigration? The Decline of the Americanization of Immigrants, 806

Tinker Guide to Latin American and Caribbean Policy and Scholarly Resources in Metropolitan New York, 118

Toward a Caring Ministry: An Investigation Into the Needs and Concerns of Divorced or Separated Persons in West Indian Churches of the Greater New York Conference of Seventh-Day Adventists, 622

A Tradition Remade in Brooklyn; West Indians Prepare a Lavish, and Popular Pageant, 272

A Transnational Dialectic of Race, Class and Ethnicity: Patterns of Identities and Forms of Consciousness among Haitian Migrants in New York City, 510

Transnationalism in the Construct of Haitian Migrants' Racial Categories of Identity in New York City, 511

The Tropics in New York, 103
Trouble in Store: Behind the Brooklyn Boycott, 547
Trying Times: Haitian Youth in an Inner City High School, 450
Two Hundred Caribbean Nationals Deported Since January from New York Area, 835

U.S. Immigration Policy and the Immigrant Populations of New York, 844
U.S. Investment and Immigration from the Caribbean, 867
U.S. Policy on Caribbean Migration: A Preliminary Study, 855
U.S. Policy Toward Haitian Boat People, 1972-93, 859
U.S. Refugee Policy: African and Caribbean Effects, 834
Unbought and Unbossed, 905
Undocumented Aliens in the New York Metropolitan Area: An Exploration Into Their Social and Labor Market Incorporation, 343
The United States Government Program of Intercepting and Forcibly Returning Haitian Boat People to Haiti: Policy Implications and Prospects, 833
United States Haitian Policy: A History of Discrimination, 849
Unwelcome Immigrants: The Labor Market Experiences of 1980 (Mariel) Cuban and Haitian Refugees in South Florida, 345
Unwinding to a Caribbean Rhythm, 258

Valence of Ethnicity, Perception of Discrimination, and Self-Esteem in High Risk Minority College Students, 540
The Vincentians and Grenadians: The Role of Voluntary Associations in Immigrant Adaptation to New York City, 203
Visibility of the New Immigrants, 810
Vodou in New York City: New Creolizations: The Economizing of Ritual Time and Space in Haitian Religion, 538
Voices of a Black Nation; Political Journalism in the Harlem Renaissance, 953
Voluntary Immigration and Continuing Encounters between Blacks: The Post-Quincentary Challenge, 811
Voodoo, Rooted in World Beyond, Flourishes Anew, 206

West Indian Carnival in Brooklyn, 260
West Indian Child Fostering: Its Role in Migrant Exchanges, 623
West Indian Diaspora: Race, Ethnicity and Politics in New York City, 929
The West Indian Dilemma: Disunity, 927
The West Indian Family: Treatment Challenges, 625
West Indian Identity in the Diaspora: Comparative Perspectives, 518
West Indian Immigrants, 353
West Indian Immigrants and the United States Education Process, 418
West Indian Immigrants in New York City 1900-1952: In Conflict with the Promised Land, 528
West Indian Immigrants: Their Social Networks and Ethnic Identification, 434
West Indian Parade Returns to Fill Streets of Brooklyn, 261
West Indian Prosperity: Fact or Fiction?, 339

West Indian Radicalism in America: An Assessment of Ideologies, 911

West Indian Women of Color: The Jamaican Woman, 703

West Indians, 112

West Indians Adding Clout At Ballot Box, 941

West Indians and Afro-Americans, 543

West Indians and Afro-Americans: A Partnership, 504

West Indians in New York City and London: A Comparative Analysis, 320

West Indians in New York: Moving Beyond the Limbo Pole, 211

West Indians in the United States of America: Some Theoretical and Practical Considerations, 306

What Is the Occupational Mobility of Black Immigrants, 313

Where Caribbean Peoples Live in New York City, 210

Women's Migration and Work: The Integration of Caribbean Women into the New York City Nurse Workforce, 375

Working With West Indian Families, 609

The World of Marcus Garvey: Race and Class in Modern Society, 948

Youthful Smoking: Patterns and Relationships to Alcohol and Other Drug Use, 738

Subject Index

Note: Numbers refer to entries in the *Guide*, not to pages.

Assimilation - Ethnicity/Race
501, 502, 508, 514 524,
527, 529, 535, 536

Assimilation - Families
602, 604, 607, 608
609, 616, 620

Assimilation - New York City
208, 209, 213, 222, 226,
303, 305, 535, 656

Assimilation - Settlement Patterns
802, 812, 320, 826, 830,
848, 854

Assimilation - Students
408, 444, 446, 447, 452

Barbadians - Background Studies
124, 557

Barbadians - Community Life
210, 211, 217

Barbadians - Economic Life
302, 303, 328, 336, 383

Barbadians - Family Life
602, 614

Barbadians - Politics
930, 950

Brooklyn (New York)
- Community Life
203, 204, 210, 211
215, 216, 217, 231

Brooklyn (New York) - Crime
231, 232, 233, 234

Brooklyn (New York)
- Economic Life
302, 304, 305, 331, 351

Brooklyn (New York)
- Ethnicity/Race
502, 515, 532, 539, 546
549, 552, 555, 561, 564
570

Brooklyn (New York)
- Family Life
617, 624, 625

Brooklyn (New York)
- Health Care
713, 717, 718

Brooklyn (New York)
- Politics
902, 913, 947, 955

Brooklyn (New York)
- Settlement Patterns
802, 807, 820, 843,
845, 847, 857, 864

Children - Ethnicity/Race
523, 559, 566

Children - Family Life
601, 603, 605, 612
616, 623, 625

Children - Health Care
705, 727, 738

Children - Socioeconomic Life
237, 344, 347,
377, 377, 435

Community Organizations
- Background Studies
108, 119

Community Organizations
- Ethnicity/Race
508, 521, 531, 535, 551, 561

Community Organizations
- General Studies
203, 217, 218, 219, 222, 233

Crime - Drug Abuse
228, 230, 231, 232, 234, 236
237, 238, 239, 240, 835

Crime - Ethnicity/Race
229, 233, 235

Crime - Schools & Youth
409, 559, 617

Cultural Identity - Assmilation
512, 514, 536, 557

Cultural Identity - Community Life
213, 214, 245, 253
257, 269, 276

Cultural Traditions - Education
427, 428, 433

Cultural Traditions - General
Studies
201, 214, 218, 241, 247, 254

Cultural Traditions - Politics
914, 915, 916, 938

Discrimination - Economic Life
306, 308, 311, 316, 318
320, 338, 344, 356, 359
379

Discrimination - Education
413, 434, 448

Discrimination - Employment
311, 314, 315, 316, 325
327, 333, 335, 349, 355
356, 358

Discrimination - Ethnicity/Race
504, 506, 509, 515,
527, 528, 530, 540

Discrimination - Health Care
701, 710, 711, 712, 721

Discrimination
- Settlement Patterns
818, 826, 833, 834, 836, 838
843, 849, 851, 856, 859, 861
866, 870, 876, 884, 888

Employment - Family Life
603, 604, 612, 620

Employment - Income
314, 315, 316, 317, 318, 323

Employment - Settlement Patterns
808, 812, 821, 824, 831
843, 846, 861, 869

Employment - Statistical Analysis
309, 313, 320, 326, 332
337, 340, 342, 343, 345
346, 354, 359, 360, 361

Ethnic Conflict
- Background Studies
108, 110, 114

Ethnic Conflict - Economic Life
301, 302, 327

Ethnic Conflict - Politics
902, 904, 911, 913, 924, 928

Ethnic Conflict - Race Relations
502, 515, 525, 532, 533
543, 546, 547, 552, 553
555, 560, 563

Ethnic Identity - Community Life
211, 218, 224, 244, 249
256, 262

Ethnic Identity - Economic Life
306, 308, 381, 382

Ethnic Identity - Family Life
602, 606, 607, 608, 609
610, 611, 613, 614, 616
617, 618, 620, 621, 623
624, 625

Ethnic Identity - Health Care
702, 703, 704, 708, 716
717, 720, 722, 726, 733

Ethnic Identity - Politics
902, 913, 916, 923, 929
930, 938, 945

Ethnic Identity
- Settlement Patterns
811, 830, 882, 886

Ethnic Relations
- Background Studies
103, 110, 112
113, 114, 121

Ethnic Relations - Education
413, 427, 432, 433, 434
437, 447, 448, 454

Ethnic Relations - General Studies
203, 211, 216, 220, 262

Family Relationships
- Education
409, 412, 417, 426, 433, 434
441, 444, 445, 451, 452

Family Relationships
- General Studies
601-625

Family Relationships
- Settlement Patterns
434, 803, 812, 824, 826
842, 846, 862, 869, 887

Farm Labor
- Economic Analysis
342, 343, 364, 365, 368

Farm Labor - Health Care
372, 374, 706, 707, 736

Farm Labor - Politics
369, 868

Farm Labor

- Working Conditions
362, 363, 366, 367
370, 371, 373

Florida - Community Life
214, 227

Florida - Economic Life
342, 344, 345, 346
348, 354, 356

Florida - Education
401, 439, 440, 446

Florida - Ethnicity/Race
505, 542, 548, 553, 556, 559

Florida - Health Care
711, 715, 728, 733, 736

Florida
- Settlement Patterns
805, 814, 826, 836, 839
841, 848, 853, 856, 859
860, 866, 879, 880

Garvey (Amy Jacques)
901, 932

Garvey (Marcus)
- Background Studies
105, 112, 909, 910, 918
919, 934, 936, 939, 949
950

Garvey (Marcus) - Economics
319, 383

Garvey (Marcus) - Politics
906, 907, 911, 912, 924
928, 937, 948, 952

Haitians - Community Life
126, 243, 246, 256

Haitians - Education
- Acculturation
414, 417, 421, 423, 429
431, 436, 441, 444, 445
446, 447

Haitians - Education
- Languages
402, 404, 405, 412, 416
420, 426, 443, 451, 454

Haitians - Ethnicity/Race
510, 511, 512, 521, 529
541, 550, 551, 555, 567
568, 569, 570

Haitians - Family Life
607, 608, 616, 618, 621

Haitians - Florida
- Settlement Patterns
805, 814, 822, 839, 841
859, 866, 879, 880

Haitians - New York
- Background Studies
105, 107, 108, 109, 124

Haitians - New York
- Community Life
202, 205, 206, 207, 210
219, 243, 246, 256

Haitians - New York
- Economic Life
322, 326, 349, 351, 387

Haitians - New York
- Education
404, 420, 421, 431, 451

Haitians - New York
- Ethnicity/Race
508, 510, 511, 512, 521
535, 538, 549, 550, 555
570

Haitians - New York
 - Settlement Patterns
 802, 807, 812, 813, 820
 822, 824, 830, 842, 843
 846, 847, 872, 873

Haitians - Refugees
 - Community Life
 345, 346, 356, 619
 715, 721

Haitians - Refugees
 - Settlement Patterns
 804, 818, 822, 825, 828
 832, 833, 834, 836, 838
 841, 849

Haitians
 - Social Relationships
 202, 246, 351, 451, 508
 529, 603, 608, 616, 620
 802, 812

Haitians - Socioeconomic
 Conditions - Background
 101, 108, 109, 120

Haitians - Socioeconomic
 Conditions - Economy
 322, 344, 346, 349, 120
 820, 826, 842, 844, 846
 860, 868, 878

Harlem - Background Studies
 103, 105, 108, 112, 114

Harlem - Community Life
 215, 221, 328, 735

Harlem - Politics
 906, 911, 930, 937
 950, 955

Harlem Renaissance
 105, 113, 245, 811
 906, 909, 956, 959

Health Care - Community Life
 122, 372, 378, 386, 615, 625

Health Care - General Studies
 701-738

Housing
 126, 204, 210, 216, 222
 302, 330, 564, 802, 857

Immigration Patterns
 - Background Studies
 104, 106, 109, 111

Immigration Patterns
 - Community Life
 204, 208, 218, 275

Immigration Patterns
 - Economic Life
 321, 324, 327, 334, 340
 341, 342, 343, 345, 356
 361, 365, 379, 380, 387

Immigration Patterns
 - Ethnicity/Race
 511, 515, 535, 557
 568, 569, 570

Immigration Patterns
 - Reference Sources
 115, 116, 120, 121, 124, 125

Immigration Patterns
 - Settlement
 801-888

Immigration Policy
 - Background Studies
 106, 111, 113, 116
 117, 123, 135

Immigration Policy
 - Economic Life
 343, 365, 366, 371

376, 377, 380

Immigration Policy
- Settlement Patterns, 810

Jamaicans - Economic Life
303, 309, 315, 317, 326
330, 335, 336, 340, 341
348

Jamaicans - Economic Life
- Women
378 379, 380, 385, 386

Jamaicans - Education
410, 422, 440, 442, 452, 453

Jamaicans - Ethnicity/Race
516, 545, 562, 570

Jamaicans - Settlement Patterns
806, 814, 819, 823, 843
862, 863, 868, 872, 873

Language Skills - Education
401, 404, 408, 411, 412
413, 415, 419, 420, 423
426, 430, 437, 442, 443
447, 449, 450, 451, 453
454

Newspapers - Politics
921, 934, 936, 937, 942, 944
952, 953, 954, 956, 959

Politics - Background Studies
105, 112, 113, 114, 117
122, 123

Politics - Community Life
203, 225, 273, 302, 334
357, 369

Politics - Economic Life
302, 334, 357, 369

Politics - Ethnicity/Race
504, 511, 520, 521, 531
532, 550, 551, 557

Politics - General Studies
901, 959

Population Statistics
- Background Studies
102, 109, 110

Population Statistics
- Community/Economy
217, 218, 259, 275
341, 343, 353

Population Statistics
- Reference Sources
124-131, 133, 134

Population Statistics
- Settlement Patterns
806, 830, 837, 845, 846
848, 858, 863, 864, 869
872, 873, 874, 887

Queens (New York)
- Community Life
105, 210

Queens (New York)
- Ethnicity/Race
517, 555, 564, 570

Queens (New York)
- Settlement Patterns
802, 807, 845, 847, 864

Religion - Community Life
112, 205, 206, 212, 219
225, 226, 227, 254

Religion - Ethnicity/Race
  502, 534, 535, 538, 549, 560

Rotating Credit Associations
  108, 112, 303, 304
  305, 330, 336

Self Concept - Ethnicity/Race
  510, 523, 526, 531
  540, 555, 557

Social Class - Community Life
  104, 112, 220, 221
  256, 325, 351

Social Class - Ethnicity/Race
  510, 539, 541, 550, 565

Social Relationships
  - Community Life
  105, 202, 220, 223, 225, 276

Socioeconomic Conditions
  - Community Life
  102, 109, 111, 212, 223

Socioeconomic Conditions
  - General Studies
  302, 304, 307, 311, 314
  325, 326, 335, 340, 343
  344, 353, 359, 360

Socioeconomic Conditions
  - Reference Sources
  126, 130, 131

Undocumented Migrants
  - Settlement Patterns
  818, 824, 838, 844
  863, 873, 884

West Indian-American Day
  Carnival
  257-277

Women - Economic Life
  326, 333, 337, 345, 360
  361, 375 - 387

Women - Family Life
  601, 603, 604, 610, 612
  620, 623

Women - Health Care
  703, 713

Women - Politics
  904, 905, 914, 922
  924, 934, 952

Women - Settlement Patterns
  812, 837, 843, 861, 869

About the Author

GUY T. WESTMORELAND, JR., is Electronic Information Services Librarian and Associate Professor at the City College of New York, a part of the City University of New York. He also compiled *An Annotated Guide to Basic Reference Books on the Black American Experience* (1974).